909 Thi

Third world

OPPOSING
VIEWPOINTS®
SERIES

The Third World

Other Books of Related Interest:

Opposing Viewpoints Series

Africa

AIDS

Democracy

Epidemics

Extremist Groups

Globalization

Global Resources

Humanity's Future

Human Rights

Obesity

Population

Poverty

Social Justice

At Issue Series

AIDS in Developing Countries

Do Infectious Diseases Pose a Serious Threat?

How Can the Poor Be Helped?

Is Poverty a Serious Threat?

Is the Gap Between the Rich and Poor Growing?

Obesity

Responding to the AIDS Epidemic

Vaccinations

What Is the State of Human Rights?

"Congress shall make no law . . . abridging the freedom of speech, or of the press."

First Amendment to the U.S. Constitution

The basic foundation of our democracy is the First Amendment guarantee of freedom of expression. The Opposing Viewpoints Series is dedicated to the concept of this basic freedom and the idea that it is more important to practice it than to enshrine it.

I The Third World

David M. Haugen, Book Editor

GREENHAVEN PRESS

An imprint of Thomson Gale, a part of The Thomson Corporation

Detroit • New York • San Francisco • San Diego • New Haven, Conn.
Waterville, Maine • London • Munich

Bonnie Szumski, *Publisher*
Helen Cothran, *Managing Editor*

For more information, contact:
Greenhaven Press
27500 Drake Rd.
Farmington Hills, MI 48331-3535
Or you can visit our Internet site at http://www.gale.com

LIBRARY OF CONGRESS CATALOGING-IN-PUBLICATION DATA

The Third World / David M. Haugen, book editor
    p. cm. -- (Opposing viewpoints)
Includes bibliographical references and index.
0-7377-2965-1 (lib. bdg.: alk. paper) 0-7377-2966-X (pbk.: alk. paper)
    1. Developing countries--Social conditions. 2. Developing countries--Economic conditions. 3. Developing countries--Foreign relations. 4. Social problems--Developing countries. 5. Economic assistance--Developing countries. I. Haugen, David M., 1969– II. Opposing viewpoints series (Unnumbered)
    HN980.T452 2006
    909'.09724083--dc22
                            2005054544

Printed in the United States of America
10 9 8 7 6 5 4 3 2 1

Contents

Chapter 3: What Is the State of Democracy in the Third World?

Chapter 4: How Should the United States Assist the Third World?

Why Consider Opposing Viewpoints?

> "The only way in which a human being can make some approach to knowing the whole of a subject is by hearing what can be said about it by persons of every variety of opinion and studying all modes in which it can be looked at by every character of mind. No wise man ever acquired his wisdom in any mode but this."
>
> John Stuart Mill

In our media-intensive culture it is not difficult to find differing opinions. Thousands of newspapers and magazines and dozens of radio and television talk shows resound with differing points of view. The difficulty lies in deciding which opinion to agree with and which "experts" seem the most credible. The more inundated we become with differing opinions and claims, the more essential it is to hone critical reading and thinking skills to evaluate these ideas. Opposing Viewpoints books address this problem directly by presenting stimulating debates that can be used to enhance and teach these skills. The varied opinions contained in each book examine many different aspects of a single issue. While examining these conveniently edited opposing views, readers can develop critical thinking skills such as the ability to compare and contrast authors' credibility, facts, argumentation styles, use of persuasive techniques, and other stylistic tools. In short, the Opposing Viewpoints Series is an ideal way to attain the higher-level thinking and reading skills so essential in a culture of diverse and contradictory opinions.

In addition to providing a tool for critical thinking, Opposing Viewpoints books challenge readers to question their own strongly held opinions and assumptions. Most people form their opinions on the basis of upbringing, peer pressure, and personal, cultural, or professional bias. By reading carefully balanced opposing views, readers must directly confront new ideas as well as the opinions of those with whom they disagree. This is not to simplistically argue that everyone who reads opposing views will—or should—change his or her opinion. Instead, the series enhances readers' understanding of their own views by encouraging confrontation with opposing ideas. Careful examination of others' views can lead to the readers' understanding of the logical inconsistencies in their own opinions, perspective on why they hold an opinion, and the consideration of the possibility that their opinion requires further evaluation.

Evaluating Other Opinions

To ensure that this type of examination occurs, Opposing Viewpoints books present all types of opinions. Prominent spokespeople on different sides of each issue as well as well-known professionals from many disciplines challenge the reader. An additional goal of the series is to provide a forum for other, less known, or even unpopular viewpoints. The opinion of an ordinary person who has had to make the decision to cut off life support from a terminally ill relative, for example, may be just as valuable and provide just as much insight as a medical ethicist's professional opinion. The editors have two additional purposes in including these lesser-known views. One, the editors encourage readers to respect others' opinions—even when not enhanced by professional credibility. It is only by reading or listening to and objectively evaluating others' ideas that one can determine whether they are worthy of consideration. Two, the inclusion of such viewpoints encourages the important critical thinking skill of objectively evaluating an author's credentials and bias. This evaluation will illuminate an author's reasons for taking a particular stance on an issue and will aid in readers' evaluation of the author's ideas.

It is our hope that these books will give readers a deeper understanding of the issues debated and an appreciation of the complexity of even seemingly simple issues when good and honest people disagree. This awareness is particularly important in a democratic society such as ours in which people enter into public debate to determine the common good. Those with whom one disagrees should not be regarded as enemies but rather as people whose views deserve careful examination and may shed light on one's own.

Thomas Jefferson once said that "difference of opinion leads to inquiry, and inquiry to truth." Jefferson, a broadly educated man, argued that "if a nation expects to be ignorant and free . . . it expects what never was and never will be." As individuals and as a nation, it is imperative that we consider the opinions of others and examine them with skill and discernment. The Opposing Viewpoints Series is intended to help readers achieve this goal.

David L. Bender and Bruno Leone,
Founders

Introduction

"To help developing countries help themselves, wealthy nations must begin to lift the burdens they impose on the poor."
—Nancy Birdsall, Dani Rodrik, Arvind Subramanian, Foreign Affairs, July/August 2005

The term *Third World* was once used to describe nations that were not aligned with the Cold War superpowers. It was never intended to be an indication of rank; instead the term referred to the one-third of the world that was not affiliated with the United States and its Western allies or the Soviet Union and the Eastern Bloc. With the collapse of the Soviet Union in 1991, however, the term has now been principally applied to countries that face extensive poverty, growing populations, and lack of industrial development. Unfortunately, such countries make up more than one-third of the globe. In fact, in scholarly debate, the Third World is often dubbed the Majority World to highlight the fact that most countries do not meet the economic output and living standards set by their industrialized counterparts.

Third World countries are located in Latin America, Africa, Asia, and the Pacific Rim. Their geographic placement primarily in the southern hemisphere has also earned them the name the "Global South"—as opposed, again, to the many developed nations in the northern hemisphere, known as the "Global North." Most Third World nations are former colonies of industrialized European countries and have a legacy of dependence on the North for governance and economic assistance. As colonies, these nations were exploited for their resources. Raw materials were mined and shipped back to European manufacturing centers, and the colonizers made few attempts to build native industries and install civic improvements on a par with European standards. When these colonies were given independence in the nineteenth and twentieth centuries, they had poor infrastructures, few trained leaders, and little technology or industrial know-how. Thus, they maintained close ties with their former rulers, bargaining resources for manufactured goods, medical supplies, and other nonnative commodities. Eventually, as they fell further behind the developed world, they looked to the industrialized nations for capital investment and loans.

In the twenty-first century, long after the supposed end of colonialism, the chains of dependency may still fetter development in the Third World. Much of the industrialized North has amalgamated, and its chief advocate and policy maker is the United States, the economically and militarily strongest of developed nations. Third World nations no longer look to their former colonizers for aid, but to the World Bank or the International Monetary Fund (IMF), lending organizations that represent the interests of the United States, the European Union, and Japan. The Third World has drawn billions of dollars from these institutions and remains heavily indebted to them. In addition, the World Bank and the IMF have been criticized for exacting stringent requirements and forcing advice upon recipient nations regarding how such funds are to be used. As Chris Brazier writes in an article in the March 2004 issue of the *New Internationalist*, "In practice governments of whatever political stripe have little alternative but to knuckle under to IMF 'advice', even if it contravenes everything they believe in." Brazier refers to the IMF's policies as a kind of fundamentalist religion that seeks to convert developing countries to its doctrine. As Brazier terms it, "The fundamentalism of the IMF lies in its religious adherence to the idea that the untrammelled free market is the solution to every economic problem."

The free market concepts employed by Western-Northern lending institutions are part and parcel of the policies of globalization, the creation of global markets in which countries can compete and hopefully push their economies forward. Since 1980, the industrialized world has put its faith in globalization to spur economic growth not only within the less-developed parts of the globe but also at home. Indeed, critics of globalization charge that this economic strategy is merely a means for rich nations to dump excess goods in Third World markets. Defenders of globalization, however, argue that entering competitive world markets has paid off for some developing countries and simply has yet to pay off for others. Most point to China as the standard bearer for globalization's benefits. As the World Bank records in its 2002 research report *Globalization, Growth, and Poverty*, China has made great strides in broaching technological, textile, and other manufacturing markets since the 1980s. The report notes that globalization has resulted in "a massive reduction in poverty" in China: "The number of rural poor in the country declined from 250 million in 1978 to just 34 million in 1999." The World Bank attests that similar changes have occurred in India, Uganda, and Vietnam as a result of taking advantage of global trade.

Some scholars refer to the Global North's shaping of Third World economies and the dictating of aid stipulations as a new form of colonialism, or neocolonialism. To them, the governments of industrialized nations care little about improving developing countries and instead are motivated to promote globalization and token foreign aid in order to gain access to natural resources and cheap labor within the Third World. According to this theory, the industrialized world relies upon vast inequalities between rich and poor in developing countries so that huge workforces can be paid a pittance to create inexpensive goods for multinational companies that sell products overseas. Defenders of globalization insist that open markets have for the most part brought greater parity between rich and poor in globalized nations. Less inequality, they argue, will eventually help developing nations to progress toward responsive and transparent government, better standards of education, less discrimination, and greater concern for human rights—all results that will put the Third World in step with the First World.

The debate over whether foreign involvement is helping or hindering the development of the Third World is considered in the following volume, *Opposing Viewpoints: The Third World*. The anthology examines this issue and other Third World concerns in chapters titled: What Problems Does the Third World Face? What Effect Is Globalization Having on the Third World? What Is the State of Democracy in the Third World? and How Should the United States Assist the Third World? The authors of the articles herein discuss how the developing world can or should be developed and whether such development is ultimately in the interests of the Third World, the First World, or perhaps both.

CHAPTER 1

What Problems Does the Third World Face?

Chapter Preface

The Third World is primarily defined by poverty. Indeed, the First and Second Worlds consist of industrialized or semi-industrialized nations that possess comparatively high standards of living, whereas most people in the Third World subsist on less than one dollar per day. One out of every six people inhabiting the planet wages a daily struggle to obtain food, clean water, adequate shelter, and health care. Most of these people live within the Third World, where inadequate resources, lack of education, unresponsive governments, and weak industries make economic advancement seem remote. Even with the commitment of First World nations to eradicate poverty on a global scale, billions of dollars in aid packages have yet to improve the lot of the majority of Third World inhabitants. In a March 2005 article in the *Times Higher Education Supplement,* economics professor William Easterly argues that foreign aid funding does little to help the impoverished masses in less developed nations because those who deliver the aid are unresponsive to the needs of the poor, and the poor have no recourse but to accept what is given to them. What aid does reach them, Easterly contends, is also probably far less than was intended because bureaucracy and corruption undoubtedly consume much of the welfare.

Not everyone, however, is as pessimistic about the future of poverty in developing nations. Some optimists point to the successful economic growth of China and India as proof that Third World nations can crawl out of the impoverishment trap. These two countries have high poverty rates yet have taken advantage of open global markets to increase per capita income. According to the World Bank, between 1980 and 2000, twenty-four developing nations entered global markets, raised manufacturing rates, and "doubled their ratio of trade to income." Many of these countries witnessed per capita growth rates of 5 percent in these decades—higher rates than many developed nations during the same time span.

Whether gains from global trade will reach the most impoverished segments of Third World populations is still a hotly debated question. As some critics contend, the higher per capita rates may just indicate that a few manufacturers are getting rich while the masses are left to their dollar-a-day existence. If this is so, it may help explain why poverty is so persistent in developing nations. And since many commentators draw connections between poverty and other social ills, the rooted nature of poverty in the Third World might explain why developing nations are host to crises in government, resource management, and health care. In the following chapter, experts examine the impact of some of these other problems that seemingly persist in—and have come to define—the Third World.

> "The bulk of the [world's] population growth will . . . accrue in the regions of the world least able to absorb large increments of people."

Overpopulation Is a Problem in the Third World

United Nations Population Fund

The United Nations Population Fund (UNFPA) is an international agency that promotes sustainable population growth. In the following viewpoint the UNFPA states that population growth is severely burdening those nations that have the least amount of resources to sustain development. The organization contends that developing nations should have more access to reproductive health services and be educated in agricultural planning and resource management. The UNFPA predicts that without these aids, overpopulated developing nations will likely face crises over food shortages, water scarcity, and other resource depletions by the mid-twenty-first century.

As you read, consider the following questions:

1. By 2050, what percentage of the world's population will crowd undeveloped countries, according to the UNFPA?

2. In the authors' view, what factors have pushed most of the world's rural poor onto low-potential land?

3. Where does the UNFPA predict the worst food insecurity will occur in the first decades of the twenty-first century?

T he world population numbered 6.3 billion in 2000 and is currently growing by a net increase of some 77 million people per year. By 2050, the United Nations Population Division, in its 2002 Revision of the world's population prospects, estimates that total world population will be 8.9 billion. The impact of this growth will be focused mainly in less developed countries, where currently some 1.2 billion people, the majority of whom are women and children, are living in extreme poverty. By mid-century, the 80 per cent share of the world's population in less developed countries in 2000, will have expanded to 88 per cent. The bulk of the population growth will thus accrue in the regions of the world least able to absorb large increments of people, threatening sustainable development and producing further deterioration in levels of living and quality of life. Without the realization of the goals of the Programme of Action of the International Conference on Population and Development (ICPD) [a 1994 gathering of 179 nations], especially universal access to gender sensitive and quality reproductive health services, it will be difficult to achieve a more favourable balance between population and available resources.

Sustainable Development

The goal is shared by millions: a better life, with a higher standard of living, education, health care and economic opportunity—not only for themselves today, but also for their children in the future. Without higher standards of living, one fifth of the world's people—including children—will continue to suffer malnutrition, disease and illiteracy. The challenge is to increase standards of living without destroying the environment.

Reproductive health and rights are integrally linked to sustainable development. Natural resources are conserved when individuals have the information and services they need to plan smaller, healthier families. And, ultimately, slowing and stabilizing the rate of population growth gives countries time to take steps that meet people's needs yet protect the environment—such as conserving fresh water, introducing more sustainable farming methods and reducing emissions of greenhouse gases.

Poverty alleviation is crucial to long-term economic and environmental sustainability. UNFPA collaborates with key partners and through integrated frameworks for development planning. North-South cooperation is vital to success in ending absolute poverty, as are fair markets, debt reduction, aid for development and foreign direct investment.

Poverty and Environmental Stress

The majority of the rural poor have increasingly become clustered on low-potential land. This outcome has resulted from a combination of factors which vary in importance from one country to another. These factors include land expropriation, demographic pressures, intergenerational land fragmentation, privatization of common lands, and consolidation and expansion of commercial agriculture with reduced labour inputs. Demographic pressures in particular continue to play an inexorable underlying role in the geographical, economic and social marginalization of the poor in most countries where there is a high incidence of poverty.

Because they have been pushed or squeezed out of high-potential land, the rural poor often have no choice but to over-exploit the marginal resources available to them through low-input, low-productivity agricultural practices such as overgrazing, soil-mining and deforestation, with consequent land degradation. Not that land degradation has been primarily instigated by poor farmers. Most deforestation has been

Toles. © 1999 by Universal Press Syndicate. Reproduced by permission.

caused by logging interests and/or rich farmers with substantial, favourable concessions. Soil erosion, water logging and salinization, which have resulted in desertification in many parts of the world, have commonly been caused by wealthy landowners with considerable financial resources.

Long-term poverty reduction and sustainable economic growth can be undermined by the degradation of the natural resource base, lack of access to and increasing scarcity of water, and air pollution that directly affect people's health and livelihoods. Opportunity declines when poor people who depend on natural resources for their livelihoods can no longer support themselves because natural resources have been damaged and they lack alternative livelihood opportunities.

Real and lasting reduction in poverty can be achieved by enhancing environmental quality and protecting human health from the adverse effects of pollution; maintaining ecosystems and improving natural resource management; securing people's access to resources; reducing people's vulnerability to environmental risks such as natural disasters; and empowering the poor by giving them a voice in decision-making.

Food and Water Security

At the turn of the century some 800 million people were undernourished owing to poverty, political instability, economic inefficiency and social inequity. The persistence of undernutrition and food insecurity in many less developed countries and the increasing scarcity and unsustainable utilization of agricultural and other environmental resources have dominated the global assessment of food and agriculture prospects. While world food production is projected to meet consumption demands for the next two decades, long-term forecasts indicate persistent and possibly worsening food insecurity in many countries, especially in sub-Saharan Africa. FAO [UN Food and Agriculture Organization] estimates that to meet the needs of a projected world population of eight billion or more in 2020, food production will have to double and it is uncertain whether that can be achieved with conventional agricultural technologies.

Many countries facing water scarcity are low-income societies that have rapidly growing populations, and are generally unable to make costly investments in water-saving technologies. Estimates indicate that over one billion people lack access to safe drinking water, and two and a half billion lack adequate sanitation. The provision of safe drinking water becomes a greater challenge as economic development and population growth place increasing demands on limited water resources. The Millennium Declaration [a UN project begun in 2000] target is to halve the proportion of people unable to reach or afford safe drinking water, between 1990 and 2015.

Women and children, especially those living in rural areas, are disproportionately affected. Rural women can spend hours everyday collecting and carting water, either from communal taps or directly from streams and rivers. Long cartage distances pose particular difficulties for elderly people and those with disabilities. Poor communities are often unable to afford the costs of maintaining pumps and boreholes, or lack the skills to do so.

Despite many problematic issues, increases in food production in some regions of the world over recent decades, suggest that the challenges of achieving food and water security throughout the world can be met. The rapid developments in the better understanding of natural resource management, combined with actual and anticipated discoveries and innovations in agricultural science, including those in biotechnology and similar areas of the knowledge revolution, offer powerful mechanisms with which to meet the on-going challenges of food security. Appropriate, integrated, social, population and sustainable development policies and programmes to empower the poorest, especially women, will support a sustainable future.

Women's Role as Resource Manager

In many less developed countries, increasing attention is being given to the critical role of women in population and environment programmes and in achieving sustainable development. Women grow a substantial proportion of the world's food, and there is considerable evidence that their labour-intensive food production practices tend to be environmentally sound, and are contributing substantially to food production while at the same time protecting the resource base.

Women make vital contributions to resource management and conservation. As resource managers, women perform various roles as: providers of food, fuel, fodder and water;

caretakers of their family's health; and conservationists (by safeguarding forests, soils, water and grazing areas). Women are key to development and therefore we must invest in their participation for sustainable development.

> "The developing world is experiencing [a rapidly ageing population], only at a far faster pace [than the industrialized world]."

Overpopulation Is Not a Problem in the Third World

Phillip Longman

Phillip Longman is a Senior Fellow at the New America Foundation, a nonpartisan policy institute in Washington, D.C. In the following viewpoint, Longman states that the world is experiencing far fewer child births each year. According to Longman, the decline is the result of many factors, including the high cost of raising children, the urbanization of populations (in which fewer children are needed to support families), and cultural ideals that equate success with smaller families. While most of such a decline can be tolerated by industrial societies, Longman argues, the dearth of children may cause difficulties in developing nations where problems such as hunger and disease are already keeping population growth in check.

As you read, consider the following questions:

1. At the dawn of the twenty-first century, how many children does the average woman bear, according to the author?

2. According to Longman, why might working women in developing countries opt not to have children?

3. In Longman's view, how will declining fertility rates affect radicalism in less developed parts of the world?

I t is not hard to understand how most of us form the impression that overpopulation is one of the world's most pressing problems. Turn on your television and you see asylum seekers slipping across border fences, or throngs of youths throwing stones somewhere in the Middle East. We hear of child soldiers in Africa, the disappearing rainforests of Brazil and melting polar ice caps—all caused by a human population that has nearly doubled in the past 40 years. We shake our heads when we read that, every year, the earth gains another 75 million human beings while losing approximately 27,000 plant or animal species.

Yet, beneath the surface of events, something else is happening. Though world population is still rising, it is doing so at barely half the rate of the late 1960s, and is now heading, many demographers believe, for absolute decline. The United Nations Population Division estimates that the number of infants and toddlers in the world (ages 0–4) will begin to contract [sometime around 2015]. The number of children under 15 will begin to decrease in little more than 20 years. This means, strange as it may sound, that all subsequent population growth will be due to increases in the numbers who survive to older ages. By 2050, there will be 35 million fewer children in the world than today, and 1.2 billion more people aged over 60.

Demographers at the International Institute for Applied Systems Analysis in Austria predict that total population will reach nine billion, mostly greying souls, by 2070 and then start to contract with compounding force. Long before then, many nations will shrink in absolute size, and the average age of the world's citizens will shoot up dramatically.

Ageing Populations

The new demographic currents in the world get stranger. During the second half of the 20th century, the median age in the UK increased by little more than three years, to 37.7. During the first half of the 21st century, according to UN forecasts, it will increase another 6.1 years. Yet this is nothing compared to the hyper ageing occurring in Iran. There, before mid-century, the median age will increase by 20 years, according to UN projections, leaving more than half the population aged over 40.

Virtually anywhere one looks in the developing world—Egypt, Iraq, Mexico—the pattern is the same. Today, televised images from China show hordes of humanity crammed into tenements or camped out in railroad stations. Yet China's working-aged population will begin to shrink within ten years. By mid-century, 30 per cent of China's population will be aged over 60, and its total population could easily be less than it was in 1980. Even Africa is ageing at nearly double the rate of the US, and during the remainder of this century it will likely grow older than Europe is today.

Countries such as Italy and Japan at least got a chance to grow rich before they grew old. Most developing countries are growing old before they get rich.

Why is this happening? The primary reason is a dramatic fall in birth rates that began in western Europe in the 1930s and is now spreading to every corner of the globe. Since the start of the 1970s, while fertility rates were falling by 27 per cent in the industrialised countries, they were plummeting by 46 per cent in what the UN terms "less developed nations". The average woman in the world now bears just 2.69 children, down from more than 4.48 in 1970. That change is sufficient to cause rapid ageing of the population, particularly in regions where fertility has fallen most dramatically, such as the Middle East. If fertility rates continue to fall, as nearly all de-

Overpopulation Is Not the Root of Development Problems

Various studies have proved that poverty and underdevelopment has no direct link to population growth per se. The causes of underdevelopment can be both internal and external. Internal causes may include poor political and economic administration, widespread corruption, excessive military budgets combined with inadequate spending on health and education, fratricidal wars, defective markets, entrepreneurial freedom erroneously understood as the right to the unbridled pursuit of profit, violations of the principle of subsidiarity, cultural-historical factors that define norms of behaviour inimical to the pursuit of integral development. To put it simply, the hungry are hungry because they are excluded from the land or cannot earn enough to survive and not because of a natural limit to the amount of food that can be produced.

Abid Ullah Jan, "Overpopulation: Myths, Facts, and Politics,"
Albalagh, July 9, 2003. http://albalagh.net/
population/overpopulation.shtml.

mographers believe they will, global population decline becomes almost inevitable.

Causes of the Drop in Child Births

It is easy to explain why children have become scarce in developed countries. In today's advanced economies, many people are not even done with school, much less established in a career, before their fertility (or their partner's) begins to decline. Then there is the rising cost of raising children. A survey found that parents in Britain spend on average £164,000 [$284,343] on each child, including the cost of university. As women have gained new economic opportunities, the costs in the form of foregone wages and compromised careers can often be even higher. Meanwhile, although social security systems around the world, as well as private pension plans, depend critically on the human capital created by parents, they offer the same pension benefits, and often more, to those who avoid the burdens of raising a family.

Now the developing world is experiencing the same demographic transition, only at a far faster pace. With the rapid growth of megacities, half the world's population now lives in urban areas, where children offer little or no economic benefit to their parents. And like their counterparts in the industrialised world, women in the third world increasingly take jobs, if only in sweatshops, and so they, too, may lose income when they bear children.

What also seems to have a dramatic effect is the availability of television. Since 1975, for example, Brazil's fertility rate has dropped by nearly half to just 2.27 children per woman. This is not the result of a family planning education programme, since Brazil has never adopted one. Instead, studies show that births have declined from one region to the next coincident with the introduction of television. Today, the number of hours that a Brazilian woman spends watching *telenovelas* (domestically produced soap operas) strongly predicts how many children she will have. These soaps, though rarely addressing reproductive issues directly, typically depict wealthy individuals living the high life in big cities. The men are dashing, lustful, power-hungry and unattached. The women are lithesome, manipulative, independent and in control of their own bodies. The few who have young children delegate their care to nannies.

The *telenovelas* thus reinforce a cultural message that is conveyed as well by many North American and western European cultural exports: that people with wealth and sophistication are people who have at most one or two children. How much television affects birth rates through such messages, and how much it does so simply by changing how men and women spend their bedtime hours, we can only speculate. The US baby boom ended the year Johnny Carson, the late-night talk show host, took to the airwaves and began attracting millions of viewers.

Some of the global fall in fertility is also no doubt a response to falling infant mortality, which means that parents don't "need" as many children to achieve their ideal family size. Yet in many parts of the world, what with AIDS, war, urban pollution and other sources of premature death, larger families are still necessary to avoid population loss. For example, in the developed world, the average woman must have about 2.1 children over her lifetime in order to replace the population, yet in war-torn Sierra Leone, 3.43 are needed. For the world as a whole, an average family size of 2.1 would lead to a 10 per cent loss of global population per generation, given current mortality rates. The spread of AIDS in countries such as India could easily make these losses still more extreme. Women who are HIV-positive suffer a dramatic decline in their ability to bear children, which is having an even more profound effect on population than the number of deaths caused by AIDS.

Benefits and Disadvantages

At first, slower population growth, and the population ageing that goes with it, seems beneficial. Many economists believe that falling birth rates helped make possible the economic boom that occurred first in Japan, and then in many other Asian nations, beginning in the 1960s. As the relative number of children declined, so did the burden of their dependency, thereby freeing up more resources for investment and adult consumption. The fall in Irish fertility rates, after birth control was legalised in 1979, produced a similar economic upturn. Today, China's rapid industrialisation is also aided by a dramatic decline in the proportion of dependent children in the population.

Over the next decade, the Middle East could benefit from a similar "demographic dividend". In every single country of that region, birth rates fell during the 1990s, often dramatically. The resulting "middle ageing" of the Middle East will ease the overall dependency ratio over the next ten to 20 years, freeing more resources for infrastructure and industrial development. With young adults accounting for a declining share of the population, the appeal of radicalism may also diminish, as Middle Eastern societies become increasingly dominated by middle-aged people concerned with such practical issues as healthcare and retirement savings. Just as population ageing in Europe in the 1990s was accompanied by the decline of the Red Brigades, the Red Army Faction and the IRA, falling birth rates in the Middle East could produce societies far less prone to political violence.

Yet even if declining fertility rates bring a "demographic dividend", that dividend eventually has to be repaid if the trend continues. At first there are fewer children to feed, clothe and educate, leaving more for adults to enjoy. But soon enough there are fewer productive workers as well, while there are also more and more dependent elderly, each of whom consumes far more resources than a child does. Even after considering the cost of education, a typical child in the US consumes 28 per cent less than the typical working-age adult, while elders consume 27 per cent more, mostly in health-related expenses. . . .

Children of the Future

So where will the children of the future come from? Some biologists speculate that modern human beings have created an environment in which the "fittest", or most successful, individuals are precisely those who have few, if any, offspring. As more and more humans find themselves living under conditions in which children, far from providing economic benefit, have become costly impediments to success, those who are well adapted to this new environment will tend not to reproduce themselves. And many others who are not so successful will imitate them.

But this hardly implies extinction. Some people will still have children. They just won't be people highly motivated by material concerns or secular values. Disproportionately, the parents of the future will be people who are at odds with the modern environment—people who either "don't get" the new rules of the game that make large families a liability or who, out of religious or chauvinistic conviction, reject the game altogether. . . .

Current demographic trends work against modernity in another way as well. Not only is the spread of urbanisation and industrialisation a major cause of falling fertility, it is a major cause of so-called "diseases of affluence", such as over-eating, lack of exercise and substance abuse, which leave an ever higher percentage of the population stricken by chronic conditions. Those who reject modernity would thus seem to have an evolutionary advantage, whether they are clean-living Mormons, or Muslims who remain committed to comparatively large families, or members of emerging sects and national movements that combine pro-natalism with anti-materialism. . . .

In his 1968 bestseller, *The Population Bomb,* Paul R. Ehrlich warned: "The battle to feed all of humanity is over. In the 1970s the world will undergo famines—hundreds of millions of people are going to starve to death in spite of any crash programmes embarked upon now." Fortunately, Ehrlich's prediction proved wrong, perhaps in part because so many people believed it would come true. But having averted the perils of overpopulation, the world now faces the unexpected challenge of population ageing and decline. We are in many ways blessed to have this problem instead of its opposite, but a problem it still is.

| "*Africa is where AIDS has entrenched itself in the last two to three decades and is still spiraling out of control.*"

AIDS Is Still Spreading in the Third World

Ed Susman

In the following viewpoint Ed Susman, a freelance writer, describes the state of the AIDS epidemic in various parts of the Third World. While the problem is serious in Asia, the Caribbean, and Latin America, Susman writes, it is especially tragic in Africa, where 26.9 million people are infected with HIV. The large number of deaths caused by the disease in Africa—especially sub-Saharan Africa—is exacting a large economic and human toll and impeding efforts to develop the region.

As you read, consider the following questions:

1. How many people were infected with HIV in 2003, according to the report cited by Susman?
2. How does AIDS affect the education system in Africa, according to Thomas Quinn, as quoted by Susman?
3. How many people are expected to have acquired HIV by 2010, according to the author?

S ometime early in the twentieth century, possibly preceding the Great Depression, a virus carried by African primates

Ed Susman, "The AIDS Epidemic Is a Serious Global Threat," *The World & I,* vol. 19, March 2004, pp. 140–47. Copyright © 2004 by News World Communications, Inc. Reproduced by permission.

jumped from one species to another, becoming HIV (human immunodeficiency virus). Fifty years later, on continents far from sub-Saharan Africa, HIV was discovered and identified as the cause of AIDS [acquired immunodeficiency syndrome].

The AIDS epidemic has become a mounting global tragedy with 20 million killed and 40 million infected. Worldwide in 2003, according to estimates from the Joint United Nations Programme on HIV/AIDS (UNAIDS), roughly five million people were infected with HIV. More than three million are expected to die from complications of the disease in 2004.

In Africa, the pandemic's effects are unmatched in their severity and tragic consequences. About 29.6 million of these infected with or dying of HIV/AIDS live in sub-Saharan Africa, where the virus spread to 3.2 million more people in 2003 alone and 58 percent of those living with HIV are women. Although the horror and extent of the disease on the African continent have brought promises of assistance from world leaders, including President George W. Bush, a combination of poverty, government inaction, myth, and stigma continues to drive the epidemic to levels that are difficult for citizens of the developed countries to comprehend.

Highly opportunistic and robust, HIV thrives and spreads among humans primarily because of promiscuous sexual behavior, unsafe medical injections, needle sharing among users of addictive drugs, mother to child transmission, and, in some parts of the world, tainted blood products. . . .

Africa

In Africa, where 16 nations have disease prevalence rates that exceed 10 percent—20 times the 0.5 percent HIV incidence rate in the United States and western Europe—many governments have ignored the epidemic that fills hospital wards and leaves millions of homeless orphans in its wake.

Nearly five million South Africans—15 percent of the population—are infected with HIV. Nevertheless, the government has for more than three years blocked efforts to provide pregnant women with drugs that can prevent transmission of HIV to their babies. It now promises that treatment programs will be in place by 2005.

It is estimated that 8,000 babies are born to HIV-infected mothers each month in South Africa. Without treatment, 33 to 40 percent of those infants will have HIV. With treatment, less than 2 percent would be born with HIV, which kills most infected babies before they are four years old.

An estimated 600 people die from AIDS every day in South Africa, and thousands more die in Botswana, Swaziland, Zimbabwe, Malawi, and all across Africa. Only in a few places are drugs being distributed; only in a few countries are preventive messages being heeded.

The Human Impact

Though these numbers are grim, the human impact behind them is numbing. As Dr. Thomas Quinn, professor of medicine at Johns Hopkins University in Baltimore, explained: "One has to consider Africa's main agricultural society. Seven million farmers have died due to AIDS. One has to ask who is farming the land.

"There is also the educational process as well as the working process," he said. "Eighty-five percent of teacher deaths in the last 20 years have been due to AIDS.

"In fact, AIDS is the leading cause of death within the continent. Because it affects many people in their young, reproductive ages, we are left with a very large number of orphans. These children are not necessarily infected with HIV but are left behind due to the premature death of their parents.

"From the global perspective the HIV epidemic has reversed many of the developmental gains that have been achieved in many areas of the world, particularly those made

A Shortage of Personnel

The single biggest obstacle to fighting AIDS in Africa, the region most laid waste by the epidemic today, is not a shortage of cash, but of personnel—doctors, nurses, pharmacists, counselors, and trained lay workers in the community. Without these people, Africa cannot even provide AIDS testing and counseling, much less antiretroviral therapy. But the only way to build up a network of health workers is to spend money—lots of it. At the hospital in Addis Ababa, Ethiopia, that serves the bulk of the country's patients on antiretroviral therapy, two doctors and two nurses care for roughly 2,000 people. By contrast, the United States employs about 15 nurses for the same number of patients. Malawi, to give another typical example from Africa, employs one nurse for every 4,000 citizens. Many countries have no doctors outside major cities and district capitals. AIDS has intensified Africa's preexisting healthcare crisis by killing off doctors and nurses and filling hospital wards, stretching healthcare even thinner. But another reason for the shortage of health professionals is that tens of thousands have emigrated.

Tina Rosenberg, Foreign Policy, *March/April 2005.*

over the last three decades," said Quinn. "There has been an economic decline, particularly on the African continent, with estimates of that decline ranging from 10 to 40 percent—a staggering figure in an area that is already economically fragile.

"One result is health-system chaos. In some places, 50 to 70 or 80 percent of hospital beds may be occupied by HIV-infected people with opportunistic infections, many of which go untreated. All of this results in a spiraling factor of political instability," Quinn noted.

"Africa is where AIDS has entrenched itself in the last two

to three decades and is still spiraling out of control. The spread of HIV continues relentlessly across the continent."

On a more positive note, he observed that some countries are making a difference in limiting its spread and in treating HIV-infected patients. Uganda, for example, has successfully reduced the incidence and prevalence of HIV through behavioral education programs, and Botswana and Senegal are implementing effective treatment programs.

Asia

While Africa's social, economic, and humanitarian catastrophe has caught the world's attention, a pending AIDS disaster in Asia barely causes a blip on the radar screen.

Officials are aware of the disease's growing incidence in India and China, which are home to more than 2 billion people. They have sounded alarms, but in vulnerable, under-educated, and poverty-stricken areas, those warnings may go unheard.

Consider India. Officially, just under 4 million people are living with HIV infection in the world's most populous democracy, but many doctors in the field think this figure is underestimated.

UNAIDS reports some progress: "New behavioral studies in India suggest that prevention efforts directed at specific populations such as female sex workers and injecting drug users are paying dividends in some states, in the form of higher HIV/AIDS knowledge and condom use.

"However," it reports, "HIV prevalence among those key groups continues to increase in some states, underlining the need for well-planned and sustained interventions on a large scale."

In neighboring Bangladesh, a nation the size of Wisconsin but with a population of 140 million, officially only a few hundred people have HIV infection, said Dr. A.Q.M. Serajul Islam, professor of dermatology and sexually transmitted diseases at Chittagong Medical College and Hospital.

"We screened 400 men at our clinic," he said, "and two of those men were positive for HIV." While that would indicate an infection rate of 0.5 percent at the clinic, Islam was more disturbed by the reactions of his patients.

"They are both married" he said, "but neither of them wanted to have his wife tested. Neither of them even wanted his wife to know that he had HIV." He said that women in Bangladesh seldom receive standard health care and rarely would receive testing for any sexually transmitted disease, let alone AIDS.

In China, which has a population of 1.3 billion, HIV infection is spreading rapidly—especially among injecting drug users. Infected blood products also are contributing to the spread of the disease there.

"The epidemic in China shows no signs of abating," the UNAIDS report stated. "Official estimates put the number of people living with HIV in China at 1 million in mid-2002. Unless effective responses rapidly take hold, a total of 10 million Chinese will have acquired HIV by the end of the decade." To put it another way, 10 million people is equivalent to the entire population of Belgium.

The Caribbean and Latin America

Although AIDS was recognized and identified in the United States and Europe in the 1980s, the extent of the disease throughout the Caribbean and Latin America is still underappreciated. According to UNAIDS: "In several Caribbean countries, adult HIV prevalence rates are surpassed only by the rates experienced in sub-Saharan Africa—making this the second-most affected region in the world."

"I don't think that the situation in Latin America and the Caribbean will ever come close to Africa, where infection rates among adults exceed 10, 15, or 20 percent. But there are already a number of countries in Latin America that have infection rates that exceed 1 percent—and that really is troublesome," said Dr. Richard Keenlyside of the Centers for Disease Control and Prevention [CDC] in Atlanta.

Reports show that the HIV infection rate is higher than 1 percent in 12 countries in the region. This might not seem very high, but at that level the disease already affects overall life expectancy and economic development.

Among the nations that have prevalence rates above 1 percent are impoverished Haiti at 6 percent and the Bahamas at 3.5 percent. Throughout the region, 1.9 million people— nearly half a million in the Caribbean—are infected with HIV.

"We are also concerned about the rising epidemic in Guyana," said Keenlyside. The small nation on South America's Caribbean shore has an HIV prevalence rate of 2.7 percent among adults between the ages of 15 and 49.

Keenlyside, associate director for external relations and public health practice for the CDC's Global AIDS Program, said he is encouraged by work being done in the Bahamas, Barbados, and Brazil.

A regional anomaly is Cuba, with an AIDS prevalence rate only one-tenth that of the United States. Cuba controls HIV spread with compulsory HIV education, generic antiretroviral drugs, and universal, mandatory testing, but Keenlyside doubts that such strict methods could be copied in democratic nations. . . .

A World at Risk

Undoubtedly, a few rays of sunshine may pierce the darkness of the HIV/AIDS pandemic, especially in the wealthier nations. For the majority of the 40 million people now infected, however—and the millions more who will become infected with the killer disease this year and next—the sunshine eludes them. Instead, the shadow of a disease that robs people of their most productive years and extends over families, communities, and nations spreads relentlessly across the landscape.

> *"[A combination of factors] portends the success of our shared efforts to limit the ravages of HIV infection and begin winning the war against AIDS."*

The Spread of AIDS Can Be Checked in the Third World

Allan R. Ronald and Merle A. Sande

Doctors Allan R. Ronald, of the University of Manitoba (Canada), and Merle A. Sande, of the University of Utah, have worked together in Uganda to combat the spread of AIDS in Africa. Along with other medical professionals working in other sub-Saharan nations, Ronald and Sande have helped increase awareness of the disease and trained staff to tend to those afflicted. As Ronald and Sande relate in the following viewpoint, the vigilant efforts of the medical community in many sub-Saharan countries—with the assistance of concerned local governments and charitable foreign organizations—has limited the spread of AIDS and benefited the lives of those who suffer from its deadly ravages.

As you read, consider the following questions:

1. As the authors explain it, what do the World Health Organization's "3 by 5" initiatives aim to accomplish?

2. According to Ronald and Sande, the success of medi-

Allan R. Ronald and Merle A. Sande, "HIV/AIDS Care in Africa Today," *Clinical Infectious Diseases,* vol. 40, 2005, pp. 1045–48. Copyright © 2005 by The University of Chicago. All rights reserved. Reproduced by permission.

cal efforts in Uganda has reduced the prevalence of
HIV infection by what percentage since 1993?

3. In the authors' experience, how have most Ugandans
responded to offers of free AIDS testing and counseling?

L ight is appearing at the end of the proverbial tunnel
throughout the regions of sub-Saharan Africa that are currently being decimated by AIDS. A remarkable congruence of
3 major streams of endeavor portends the success of our
shared efforts to limit the ravages of HIV infection and begin
winning the war against AIDS on several fronts. The first endeavor is to ensure that the incredible, indescribable plight of
individuals dying of AIDS is being heard by individuals, organizations, and governments around the world. AIDS-associated
tragedies, such as the 8000 deaths that occur each day, the fact
that a new child is orphaned every 14 s[econds], and the col-
lapsing of economies, have raised the topic of AIDS to the
forefront of the global conscience. As a result, the world is
rolling up its sleeves and is beginning to respond. The "3 by
5" initiatives of the World Health Organization have set forth
the goal that 3 million HIV-infected individuals in developing
countries will be receiving antiretroviral [drug] treatment by
31 December 2005. A second endeavor is the opportunity to
make a difference for sick, frequently impoverished patients
with AIDS who are awaiting death. Although, in the West, we
have only prescribed antiretrovirals effectively since 1996, we
already know that the vast majority of HIV-infected individuals—presumably, almost 90% of such individuals—can remain well and can fulfill their desires and responsibilities
within the home, workplace, and community for at least 5
years thanks to these complex but life-sustaining regimens.
The world has found multiple ways to bring the cost of antiretrovirals into a reasonable price range. Finally, a third endeavor, which is equally important but is readily forgotten, is

the success story that has unfolded in Uganda, where the prevalence and incidence of HIV infection have been dramatically reduced. This endeavor provides hope that, collectively, individuals and societies can change behaviors, reduce risks, and alter transmission dynamics so that, even in the absence of an AIDS vaccine, marked reductions in the global incidence of HIV infection will occur within the next 5 years.

Cooperative Efforts

In their [2005] report, [C.W.] Wester et al. summarized [in *Clinical Infectious Diseases*] the lessons that they have learned from their experiences with the antiretroviral treatment clinic established through the auspices of the Botswana-Harvard School of Public Health AIDS Initiative Partnership for HIV Research and Education in Gaborone, Botswana. They also reported an important innovation in the fight against HIV/AIDS in Africa: the public-private partnership (in this case, a partnership involving The Merck Company Foundation/Merck & Company, the Bill & Melinda Gates Foundation, Harvard University, and the government of Botswana). The lessons learned from their experiences, our own experiences, and experiences at sites elsewhere in sub-Saharan Africa need to be assimilated, and dozens of sites for HIV/AIDS care need to be developed, with the goal of achieving the 3 by 5 targets of the World Health Organization through the cooperative efforts and largess of the global society.

The Academic Alliance for AIDS Care and Prevention in Africa Foundation is a similar public-private partnership that was created in 2000 as a partnership between Ugandan and North American physicians in academic medicine, Pfizer Pharmaceuticals and the Pfizer Foundation, and the Makerere University Faculty of Medicine and Mulago Hospital in Kampala, Uganda. With a firm handshake and the blessing of Ugandan President Yoweri Musevani, the Uganda Ministry of Health, and the Uganda AIDS Commission, the consortium began to

The Clinton Initiative to Fight AIDS Worldwide

The Clinton HIV/AIDS Initiative works with governments to develop and implement operational business plans for large-scale, comprehensive prevention, care and treatment programs. . . .

The Initiative is committed to providing long-term assistance in each country it works with. However, the ultimate goal is to diminish its role over time as the country develops the capacity to administer all necessary programs on its own. As such, program management and sustainability are emphasized throughout this process. Countries take the lead, and the Foundation continues to provide technical assistance as needed. The goal is to develop effective models in the affected countries, so that other countries and international agencies can then use them as guides in implementing their own programs.

Ira Magaziner, Brown Journal of World Affairs, *Summer/Fall 2004.*

build its programs in June 2001. In early 2002, expanded clinics were opened, and a 4-week physician-training course was organized and taught in partnership and cooperation with trainers from the Infectious Diseases Society of America. Our experiences were similar to those in Botswana. Our limited facilities at Mulago Hospital . . . were quickly overwhelmed, and sick patients who required care appeared from everywhere. Most patients were poor, and many were illiterate. Within 3 years, [more than] 8000 HIV-infected individuals have been registered in our adult and pediatric clinics. . . .

We were fortunate to work within a society that has created a substantial infrastructure for the prevention of HIV infection, albeit an infrastructure that is less developed for the treatment and care of patients with HIV infection. The prevalence of HIV infection has decreased by [more than] 50% during the past 12 years; this decrease in prevalence has been accompanied by a decrease in the incidence of HIV infection, particularly among patients in younger age groups (i.e., patients [less than] 20 years of age). Expanded access to care ideally should occur in a setting in which prevention is a primary priority of both the government and the organizations responsible for program delivery. The reasons underlying the success achieved in Uganda are still being debated, but they include inspired presidential leadership; emphasis on the "ABC's" (i.e., Abstinence, Be faithful [or "zero grazing"], and Condom access for risky behaviors); processes that facilitated the emergence of [more than] 2000 nongovernmental organizations, including initiatives by religious organizations; limited controversy with regard to promotion of condom use; and reduced stigma because of societal acceptance of HIV infection as a diagnosis and of AIDS as a cause of death. Other countries, presumably including Botswana, are also expanding programs that will reduce the incidence of HIV infection. . . .

What Needs to Be Done

Now we need a sustained commitment from leadership to provide enhanced care for individual patients with AIDS, including access to antiretroviral treatment. Few countries have made significant revisions of their national budgets or, even, their national priorities to address issues of care. In societies devastated by AIDS, there has been little serious preparation by most governments, universities, or health care institutions to prepare to meet the massive human and fiscal resources required to provide even limited programs of HIV/AIDS care. . . .

"Business as usual" will not suffice if we wish to take advantage of the billions of monies available to provide HIV/AIDS care and reduce by 50% the number of deaths due to AIDS that will otherwise occur between now and 2010. Organizational structures must be renewed, and there must be a sustained, serious commitment of national and institutional leadership to rapidly deploy both the human and fiscal resources necessary for this massive public undertaking. Care and prevention organizations that demonstrate effective and efficient financial structures, as well as accountability, must be rewarded with available resources that can be deployed to patient care quickly and effectively.

In Botswana, Wester et al. also identified the need to build treatment capacity with additional trained human resources. At our site, we have trained 300 physicians to train other physicians to become trainers themselves, including 68 physicians from 13 African countries outside Uganda. These individuals have been tasked and have been given the skill set to provide training when they return to their own environment. Although monitoring/evaluation processes are only now in place to critically assess the effectiveness of the training program, we sense that most of the trainees have the capacity to deliver competent HIV/AIDS care. . . .

Tragically, [less than] 10% of HIV-infected Africans know their HIV infection status. We have introduced voluntary counseling and testing into the medical wards of Mulago Hospital, where the prevalence of HIV infection is [more than] 65%, and we have found that (1) most patients accept testing when it is offered freely, and (2) they are prepared to enter care programs. With the support of external funding from the Bill & Melinda Gates Foundation, we have been able to demonstrate the acceptability of voluntary counseling and testing, and, with the use of funds from the President's Emergency Plan for AIDS Relief, such services are being widely implemented in Uganda. . . .

Positive Signs

Adequate adherence to antiretroviral treatment has been presumed to be difficult to achieve within Africa. Fortunately, all studies that have appeared to date have suggested that, with appropriate training, motivation, and supervision, adherence will be possible. This does not imply that adherence will be "easy" to achieve. Although HIV prevention must remain the first priority of all of us who are working in the field of HIV/AIDS care, prevention of the development of resistance [to antiretroviral drugs] among HIV isolates [those in care] is a close second within Africa. We have demonstrated that, in our patients in Kampala, the development of resistance among HIV isolates is most likely to occur in patients who miss drug doses for [more than] 2 days. Close monitoring and counseling regarding the use of antiretrovirals must ensure that these "drug holidays" are minimized. . . .

Finally, public-private partnerships (such as the program in Botswana discussed in the report by Wester et al. and our own Academic Alliance Program in Uganda) have the potential to make enormous contributions to the fight against HIV/AIDS in Africa and elsewhere. However, as we work together to create and scale up care and prevention programs, it is essential to monitor and evaluate the effectiveness of such programs. Donors, including the US Government, as well as the governments of host countries, should insist on documentation of the results of their investments and evidence of the effective use of antiretroviral drugs, including measures of adherence, prevention of resistance, and management of side effects, as well as implementation of prevention initiatives and sustainability of productive lives. Only programs that can achieve those goals and document the results should continue to be eligible for funding.

In summary, many lessons can be learned from the experiences of the alliances that are being formed between HIV caregivers in Africa and in Western countries. To paraphrase Winston Churchill during the early days of World War II, "We have not reached the beginning of the end, but perhaps we are approaching the end of the beginning."

"As of July 2004, 35 countries faced food crises requiring emergency assistance."

Hunger Is a Problem in the Third World

Food and Agriculture Organization of the United Nations

The Food and Agriculture Organization of the United Nations (FAO) monitors world food scarcity and cooperates with national governments on agriculture improvement plans. Every year the FAO publishes a report titled "The State of Food Insecurity in the World." In the following viewpoint, taken from the 2004 report, the FAO maintains that food scarcity and malnutrition still plague many developing nations. The costs of such widespread hunger, the FAO states, are lost productivity, underdeveloped children, and high rates of mortality.

As you read, consider the following questions:

1. According to the FAO, how many years of "productive life" are lost in the developing world due to malnutrition?

2. What fraction of the number of babies born in developing nations is born stunted, in the FAO's assessment?

3. What are some of the indirect costs of hunger in de-

Food and Agriculture Organization of the United Nations, "The State of Food Insecurity in the World, 2004," www.fao.org, 2004.

veloping nations, according to the FAO, and how much are they costing developing economies?

FAO estimates that 852 million people worldwide were undernourished in 2000-2002. This figure includes 815 million in developing countries, 28 million in the countries in transition and 9 million in the industrialized countries.

The number of undernourished people in developing countries decreased by only 9 million during the decade following the World Food Summit baseline period of 1990-1992. During the second half of the decade, the number of chronically hungry in developing countries increased at a rate of almost 4 million per year, wiping out two thirds of the reduction of 27 million achieved during the previous five years.

Trends Around the World

The reversal during the second half of the decade resulted mainly from changes in China and India. China had registered dramatic progress during the first half of the decade, reducing the number of undernourished by almost 50 million. During the same period, India pared the number of undernourished by 13 million. Gains in these two countries drove the global totals down, despite the fact that the number of undernourished in the rest of the developing world increased by 34 million. During the second half of the decade, however, progress slowed in China, where the number of undernourished fell by only 4 million. In India the number increased by 18 million.

The news is not all bad, however. Just as gains in China and India outweighed setbacks elsewhere during the first half of the decade, the slowdown in the two Asian giants masked significant improvements in trends for the rest of the developing world. After climbing at a rate of almost 7 million per year, the number of undernourished in developing countries other than China and India essentially held steady during the second half of the decade. And the proportion of people who were undernourished declined from 20 percent to 18 percent.

Encouragingly, the most pronounced change in trends took place in sub-Saharan Africa. Between 1995-1997 and 2000-2002, the rate of increase in the number of undernourished slowed from 5 million per year to 1 million per year. And the proportion of undernourished in the region fell from 36 percent, where it had hovered since 1990-1992, to 33 percent.

The Impact of Hunger on Children

Hunger and malnutrition inflict heavy costs on individuals and households, communities and nations. Undernourishment and deficiencies in essential vitamins and minerals cost more than 5 million children their lives every year, cost households in the developing world more than 220 million years of productive life from family members whose lives are cut short or impaired by disabilities related to malnutrition, and cost developing countries billions of dollars in lost productivity and consumption.

Every year, more than 20 million low birthweight (LBW) babies are born in the developing world. In some countries, including India and Bangladesh, more than 30 percent of all children are born underweight.

From the moment of birth, the scales are tipped against them. LBW babies face increased risk of dying in infancy, of stunted physical and cognitive growth during childhood, of reduced working capacity and earnings as adults and, if female, of giving birth to LBW babies themselves.

Compared with normal babies, the risk of neonatal death is four times higher for infants who weigh less than 2.5 kilograms at birth and 18 times higher for those who weigh less than 2.0 kilograms. LBW babies also suffer significantly higher rates of malnutrition and stunting later in childhood and as adults. A study in Guatemala found that by the time they reached adolescence LBW boys were 6.3 centimetres shorter and 3.8 kilograms lighter than normal, while girls lost 3.8 centimetres in height and 5.6 kilograms in weight.

Stunting and Malnutrition

Almost one third of all children in developing countries are stunted, with heights that fall far enough below the normal range for their age to signal chronic undernutrition. Stunting, like LBW, has been linked to increased illness and death, to reduced cognitive ability and school attendance in childhood and to lower productivity and lifetime earnings in adults. . . .

Overall, the World Health Organization (WHO) estimates that more than 3.7 million deaths in 2000 could be attributed to underweight. Deficiencies in three key micronutrients— iron, vitamin A and zinc—each caused an additional 750,000 to 850,000 deaths.

A study of trends in malnutrition and child mortality in 59 developing countries between 1966 and 1996 found that reducing levels of underweight had a significant effect on reducing child mortality, regardless of other socioeconomic and policy changes. . . .

Effects on Productivity and Prosperity

Estimating the millions of human lives cut short or scarred by disability leaves no doubt that hunger is morally unacceptable. Calculating the value of lost productivity in dollars suggests that allowing hunger to persist is simply unaffordable, not only to the victims themselves but to the economic development and prosperity of the nations in which they live.

The costs of hunger to society come in several distinct forms. Perhaps the most obvious are the direct costs of dealing with the damage it causes. These include the medical costs of treating both the problem pregnancies and deliveries of anaemic, underweight mothers and the severe and frequent illnesses of children whose lives are threatened by malaria, pneumonia, diarrhoea or measles because their bodies and immune systems have been weakened by hunger.

Table 1. Characteristics of More Globalized and Less Globalized Developing Economies

Population-Weighted Averages

Socioeconomic characteristics	More globalized (24)	Less globalized (49)
Poplulation, 1997	2,900,000,000	1,100,000,000
Per capita GDP, 1980	$1,488	$1,947
Per capita GDP, 1997	$2,485	$2,133
Inflation, 1980	16%	17%
Inflation, 1997	6%	9%
Rule of law index 1997 (world average = 0)	-0.04	-0.48
Average year primary schooling, 1980	2.4	2.5
Average year primary schooling, 1997	3.8	3.1
Average year secondary schooling, 1980	0.8	0.7
Average year secondary schooling, 1997	1.3	1.3
Average year tertiary schooling, 1980	0.08	0.09
Average year tertiary schooling, 1997	0.18	0.22

SOURCE: D. Dollar, World Bank research paper, 2001.

A very rough estimate, apportioning medical expenditures in developing countries based on the proportion of disability-adjusted life years (DALYs) attributed to child and maternal undernutrition, suggests that these direct costs add up to around US$30 billion per year—over five times the amount committed so far to the Global Fund to Fight AIDS, Tuberculosis and Malaria.

These direct costs are dwarfed by the indirect costs of lost productivity and income caused by premature death, disabil-

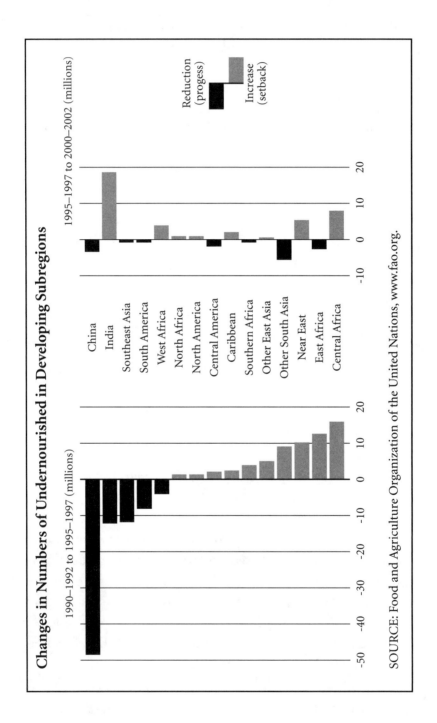

Changes in Numbers of Undernourished in Developing Subregions

1990–1992 to 1995–1997 (millions)

1995–1997 to 2000–2002 (millions)

China
India
Southeast Asia
South America
West Africa
North Africa
North America
Central America
Caribbean
Southern Africa
Other East Asia
Other South Asia
Near East
East Africa
Central Africa

Reduction (progess)

Increase (setback)

SOURCE: Food and Agriculture Organization of the United Nations, www.fao.org.

ity, absenteeism and lower educational and occupational opportunities. Provisional estimates suggest that these indirect costs range into the hundreds of billions of dollars.

Both the direct and indirect costs represent the price of complacency, of allowing widespread hunger to persist. Both are unacceptably high, not only in absolute terms but in comparison with estimates of a third type of costs—the costs of interventions that could be taken to prevent and eliminate hunger and malnutrition. Numerous studies suggest that every dollar invested in well-targeted interventions to reduce undernourishment and micronutrient deficiencies can yield from five times to over 20 times as much in benefits. . . .

Hunger Hotspots

As of July 2004, 35 countries faced food crises requiring emergency assistance. Neither the number of crises nor their locations differed markedly from the situation reported in "The State of Food Insecurity in the World 2003." Most of the crises were concentrated in Africa and were caused by drought, conflict or a combination of the two. Almost all had persisted over a prolonged period, with an average duration of nine years.

In East Africa alone, the food security of over 13 million people was threatened by a combination of erratic rains and the impact of recent and ongoing conflicts. Escalating civil conflict in the Darfur region of the Sudan uprooted more than a million people from their homes and fields, precipitating a major crisis. Elsewhere in the subregion, recurrent drought caused crop failures and heavy livestock losses in parts of Ethiopia, Eritrea, Somalia, Uganda and Kenya.

The number of food emergencies has been rising over the past two decades, from an average of 15 per year during the 1980s to more than 30 per year since the turn of the millennium. Most of this increase has taken place in Africa, where the average number of food emergencies each year has almost tripled.

The balance of causes of food emergencies has also shifted over time. Since 1992, the proportion of emergencies that can be attributed mainly to human causes, such as conflict or economic failures, has more than doubled, rising from around 15 percent to more than 35 percent.

In many cases, natural and human-induced factors reinforce each other. Such complex crises tend to be the most severe and prolonged. Between 1986 and 2004, 18 countries were "in crisis" more than half of the time. War or economic and social disruptions caused or compounded the crises in all 18. These countries also offer evidence that frequent and prolonged crises cause widespread chronic undernourishment. FAO's latest estimates list 13 of the 18 countries among those where more than 35 percent of the population goes hungry.

| "The fraction of overweight and obese people is growing at alarming rates in many developing countries."

Obesity Is a Problem in the Third World

Lila Guterman

In the following viewpoint Lila Guterman reports that developing nations—hounded perennially by malnutrition—are now struggling with another food-related problem, obesity. According to Guterman and her sources, the chief causes of obesity are the introduction of Western diets that are high in fat and the movement of more people to urban centers where sedentary lifestyles replace the physical demands of rural living. Lila Guterman is a science writer based in Washington, D.C. She writes for the Chronicle of Higher Education.

As you read, consider the following questions:

1. What obesity-related diseases have shot up in developing countries in recent years, according to Barry M. Popkin, as cited by the author?

2. As Marquisa La Velle, as cited by Guterman, explains, how has unemployment contributed to obesity among aboriginal tribes of Australia?

Lila Guterman, "Obesity Problem Swells Worldwide," *Chronicle of Higher Education,* vol. 48, March 8, 2002, p. A18. Copyright © 2002 by the *Chronicle of Higher Education.* This article may not be published, reposted, or redistributed without express permission.

> 3. According to Stanley J. Ulijaszek, quoted by the author, why are people in remote areas of Papua New Guinea gaining weight?

Many people think of obesity as a Western problem, a disease of affluence. But some researchers have found that people around the world are getting fatter, including those in developing countries who until recently faced only one dietary problem: malnutrition.

Now a sedentary lifestyle and the Western diet, high in fat and low in carbohydrates, are permeating some of the world's most remote places. Researchers outlined the growing international epidemic of obesity [in February 2002] at a symposium at the annual conference [in Washington, D.C.,] of the American Association for the Advancement of Science.

"The recognition that this is a worldwide problem is very recent," said Marquisa La Velle, a biological anthropologist at the University of Rhode Island.

The Nutrition Transition

Barry M. Popkin, a professor of nutrition at the University of North Carolina at Chapel Hill, called the pattern of changing dietary habits "the nutrition transition." He said that the problems of undernourishment, such as stunted childhood growth, infections, and vitamin deficiencies, are quickly being replaced by the diseases that accompany obesity: high blood pressure, cancer, heart disease, and diabetes. He said "a very fine line" separates a diverse, healthy diet and one that provides too many calories or too much fat and that leads to disease. Already the number of new cases of diabetes in India and China annually outpaces the rest of the world put together.

Mr. Popkin summarized the results of an international meeting . . . in Italy, where nutrition researchers presented evidence that the fraction of overweight and obese people is growing at alarming rates in many developing countries. (People are defined as overweight or obese if their body-mass indexes are higher than 25 and 30, respectively. A person's body-mass index equals his weight in kilograms divided by the square of his height in meters.) In some countries, particularly in the Middle East and Pacific islands, a larger percentage of the population is overweight or obese than in the United States, where 61 percent of adults exceed healthy weights.

In many countries, the numbers are skyrocketing. In Mexico, 60 percent of women were overweight or obese in a 1999 study and an additional 2.4 percent join those categories each year, compared with about one-quarter of 1 percent of the U.S. population. In Thailand, 13 percent of men and 25 percent of women were already overweight or obese in 1996, and 1.1 percent more men and 1.8 percent more women enter the heavy ranks every year.

Not Just the Affluent

Previous research had documented that wealthier people tend to be fatter than poorer people in developing countries. But what was once an affliction of affluence is no longer. In a 1997 survey in Brazil, the high-income groups consumed less sugar and more vegetables than lower-income people, and had lower body-mass indexes. "In some parts of the world, the burden [of obesity] is shifting toward the poor," Mr. Popkin said.

The pattern is not a simple one, however. Ms. La Velle was surprised at how little socioeconomic status affected levels of obesity in two groups of children she studied in South Africa. With Maciej Henneberg, the head of the department of anatomical sciences at Australia's University of Adelaide, she measured heights and weights of more than 600 children, half living in Cape Town and the other half in a rural community 200 miles to the east, called Klein Karoo.

They found that children whose parents had higher-paying jobs and more education did tend to weigh more than their

New Health Risks for Developing Nations

The knock-on [secondary] effects of . . . weight gain on patterns of disease [in developing countries] will be dramatic. Diabetes, heart disease and other so-called "diet-related non-communicable diseases" will join the list of ailments straining the public-health facilities of poor countries, many of which are still engaged in fighting off diseases such as malaria and tuberculosis. The number of new cases of adult-onset diabetes in China and India already exceeds new cases in the whole of the rest of the world. An epidemic of cardiovascular disease lies heartbeats away.

Economist, *February 23, 2002.*

poorer counterparts in each location. But the difference in locale had a much greater effect. The urban children were fatter than the rural ones, with 16 percent of Cape Town boys and 12 percent of the girls obese, compared with 1 percent of the boys and 1.6 percent of the girls in Klein Karoo.

The Effects of Culture

Patterns of obesity vary from one site to another, depending on the prevailing culture, Ms. La Velle said. When she turned to a group of aborigines living in the central Australian desert, she found underfed, stunted, physically active children and obese, sedentary adults. In that area, 95 percent of the adults were unemployed and inactive, she said. "Very small children [are] all of a sudden exploding into obese adults," she said.

Stanley J. Ulijaszek, an anthropologist at the University of Oxford, found that the heaviest people in an extremely remote area of Papua New Guinea, called the Purari Delta, were those who had urban connections—they had relatives who lived in cities or they had visited urban locations elsewhere in the country. In the Purari Delta, which is reachable only by light aircraft followed by a two-hour ride in a dugout canoe, Mr. Ulijaszek said, sugar and cooking oil are available in trading posts. He said: "The people who are buying this stuff have some sense of what people are doing in towns." As a result, 1 percent of men and 5 percent of women in the Purari Delta are now obese, an increase from a total absence of fatness 20 years ago.

Searching for Solutions

There are no easy solutions to obesity, as many Westerners know from personal experience. Although she recommended building more physical activity into people's lives, regardless of location, Ms. LaVelle stressed that the varying cultures should influence strategies to combat obesity, just as those cultures helped create the problem.

In papers that were just published in *Public Health Nutrition* about [the 2001] international conference, researchers presented the success stories of a few countries. In South Korea, housewives learn to cook the traditional low-fat, high-vegetable cuisine, and as a result, obesity is much lower there than if they had adopted Western foods, according to Mr. Popkin. Finland has instituted national pricing and food-labeling programs to promote healthy diets. Brazil has started a mass-media campaign to educate people about healthy diets, and requires fresh fruits and vegetables in government-sponsored lunches for schoolchildren.

Without such success at prevention, the public-health costs of obesity will soar, the speakers warned. . . . Part of the problem is the speed of the increase in obesity, Mr. Popkin said. The United States and Europe experienced the transition relatively slowly, allowing public-health authorities more time to gear up to treat obesity-related diseases. But in the developing world, the transition is taking place "overnight," he said. Some countries have been "dealing with hunger and undernutrition, and all of a sudden they have half the population overweight and obese, and they have diabetes and stroke."

Said Ms. La Velle, "This puts a burden on the developing world that it can ill afford."

Periodical Bibliography

The following articles have been selected to supplement the diverse views presented in this chapter.

Makoto Atoh	"The Current State of World Population: A North-South Contrast," *Asia-Pacific Review*, November 2000.
Economist	"More or Less Equal?" March 13, 2004.
Noreena Hertz	"Now Is the Time to Act," *New Statesman*, July 4, 2005.
Richard Kim	"Bush and AIDS," *Nation*, February 24, 2003.
John Knodel and Mary Beth Ofstedal	"Gender and Aging in the Developing World: Where Are the Men?" *Population & Development Review*, December 2003.
Lancet	"Predicting the Failure of 3 by 5," May 7, 2005.
Ira Magaziner	"Scaling-Up Care and Treatment for People Living with HIV and AIDS in the Developing World," *Brown Journal of World Affairs*, Summer/Fall 2004.
Shelley Page	"Safe No More," *Ottawa (Canada) Citizen*, October 24, 2004.
Andrew C. Revkin	"The Future of Calamity," *New York Times*, January 2, 2005.
Christopher D. Ringwald	"The Danger of Good Intentions," *National Catholic Reporter*, May 13, 2005.
Richard Rothstein	"Defending Sweatshops," *Dissent*, Spring 2005.
Jeffrey D. Sachs	"Can Extreme Poverty Be Eliminated?" *Scientific American*, September 1, 2005.
Pedro A. Sanchez and M.S. Swaminathan	"Cutting World Hunger in Half," *Science*, January 21, 2005.

CHAPTER 2

What Effect Is Globalization Having on the Third World?

Chapter Preface

In the last two decades of the twentieth century, several Asian nations—including China, India, South Korea, Thailand, Malaysia, and Indonesia—reaped the benefits of globalization, the opening of markets and lowering of protective barriers (such as tariffs) to global trade. In these developing countries exports rose and manufacturing became a larger and more important sector of their economies. In addition, information technologies helped increase technical communications between industrialized nations and these less-developed Asian counterparts, and airfreight allowed them to compete in global markets with their relatively inexpensive wares. As economics professor David Bigman writes in *Globalization and the Developing Countries*, "Most East Asian countries enjoyed rapid growth as they increased their trade with and their integration into the global markets; the structural changes that spurred this growth improved their standard of living and elevated a large number of their people out of poverty."

However, this globalization boon did not positively impact all of the Third World, according to Bigman. He notes that many developing countries, especially in sub-Saharan Africa, "have so far benefited very little and are becoming increasingly marginalized." Bigman and other critics of globalization argue that nations with largely agricultural economies have difficulty taking advantage of world markets, which are hungry for manufacturing and technological products. When globalization policies are visited upon traditional, agriculture-based nations, the push toward industry tends to force people to uproot from rural settings and migrate to cities where they become a vast pool of unskilled labor. Devoid of their native community support systems and facing increased urban living costs, many of these people sink deeper into poverty instead of rising up out of it. Furthermore, these critics contend, improving economies may not better people's lives if other factors such as weak government, ethnic strife, or war are still entrenched in Third World nations.

What most advocates and critics concede is that globalization has had a varied impact upon the diverse geographies of the Third World. However, as the viewpoints in the following chapter reveal, this conclusion does not deter advocates of globalization policies from insisting that opening up developing economies will in the long run improve the lot of most impoverished nations. It also does not dissuade detractors from cautioning that the dark side of globalization may eclipse any benefits and further separate the haves from the havenots.

> "Opening up [trade] integrates an
> economy into a larger market, and
> . . . the size of the market matters
> for growth."

Globalization Helps Nations Develop

The World Bank

With over 180 member nations, the World Bank is an international institution that raises money and lends it to developing countries. In the following viewpoint, the World Bank argues that globalization—the opening up of markets and avenues of communication between countries—generally benefits developing parts of the world. Although the bank cautions that liberalized trade is not a panacea for struggling nations, many developing countries that have broken into global markets have increased exports, improved business infrastructure, and bettered social services such as education and health care due to rising capital.

As you read, consider the following questions:

1. According to the World Bank, manufactured products were what percentage of exports from developing countries in 1998 as compared to 1980?

2. In the World Bank's view, a rise in education standards in developing countries tends to affect what two

other social arenas?

3. What outcomes does the World Bank claim are spurred by a developing nation entering into a large global market?

T he new [third] wave of globalization, which began about 1980, is distinctive. First, and most spectacularly, a large group of developing countries broke into global markets. Second, other developing countries became increasingly marginalized in the world economy and suffered declining incomes and rising poverty. Third, international migration and capital movements, which were negligible during second wave globalization [during the Industrial Revolution], have again become substantial. . . .

The Changing Structure of Trade: The Rise of the New Globalizers

The most encouraging development in third wave globalization is that some developing countries, accounting for about 3 billion people, have succeeded for the first time in harnessing their labor abundance to give them a competitive advantage in labor-intensive manufactures and services. In 1980 only 25 percent of the exports of developing countries were manufactures; by 1998 this had risen to 80 percent. . . .

This is an astonishing transformation over a very short period. The developing countries that have shifted into manufactures trade are quite diverse. Relatively low-income countries such as China, Bangladesh, and Sri Lanka have manufactures shares in their exports that are above the world average of 81 percent. Others, such as India, Turkey, Morocco, and Indonesia, have shares that are nearly as high as the world average. Another important change in the pattern of developing country exports has been their substantial increase in exports of services. In the early 1980s, commercial services made up 17 percent of the exports of rich countries but only 9 percent of the exports of developing countries. During the third wave of globalization the share of services in rich country exports increased slightly—to 20 percent—but for developing countries the share almost doubled to 17 percent.

What accounted for this shift? Partly it was changing economic policy. Tariffs on manufactured goods in developed countries continued to decline, and many developing countries undertook major trade liberalizations. At the same time many countries liberalized barriers to foreign investment and improved other aspects of their investment climate. Partly it was due to continuing technical progress in transport and communications. Containerization and airfreight brought a considerable speeding up of shipping, allowing countries to participate in international production networks. New information and communications technologies mean it is easier to manage and control geographically dispersed supply chains. And information based activities are "weightless" so their inputs and outputs (digitized information) can be shipped at virtually no cost. . . .

The More Globalized Developing Countries

By the end of the millennium economic activity was highly concentrated geographically. . . . Africa has a very low output density and this is unlikely to change through a uniform expansion of production in every location. Africa has the potential to develop a number of successful manufacturing/service agglomerations [clustered and related businesses], but if its development is like that of any other large region, there will be several such locations around the continent and a need for labor to migrate to those places. Africa is much less densely populated than Europe, and the importance of migration to create agglomerations is therefore greater.

However, most countries are not just victims of their location. The newly globalizing developing countries helped their firms to break into industrial markets by improving the complementary infrastructure, skills and institutions that modern production needs. So, to some extent these developing countries that broke into world markets just happened to be well located and to some extent they shaped events by their own actions. To get some understanding of this distinction it is useful to look at the characteristics of the post-1980 developing globalizers. We rank developing countries by the extent to which they increased trade relative to income over the period, and compare the top third with the remaining two-thirds. The one-third/two-thirds distinction is of course arbitrary. We label the top third "more globalized" without in any sense implying that they adopted pro-trade policies. The rise in trade may have been due to other policies or even to pure chance. By construction, the "more globalized" had a large increase in trade relative to income: 104 percent, compared to 71 percent for the rich countries. The remaining two-thirds of developing countries have actually had a decline in trade [relative] to GDP [gross domestic product] over this period. . . .

The more globalized were not drawn from the higher-income developing countries. Indeed, in 1980 they were poorer as a group. The two groups had very similar educational attainment in 1980. Since 1980, the more globalized have made very significant gains in basic education: the average years of primary schooling for adults increased from 2.4 years to 3.8 years. The less globalized made less progress and now lag behind in primary attainment. The spread of basic education tends to reduce inequality and raise health standards, as well as being complementary to the process of raising productivity. It can also be seen in that both groups reduced inflation to single digits over the past two decades. Finally, as of 1997 the more globalized fared moderately better on an index of property rights and the rule of law. The same measure is not available for 1980, but clearly countries such as China and Hungary have strengthened property rights as they have reformed.

The Effects of Policy Changes

During third wave globalization, the new globalizers also cut import tariffs significantly, 34 points on average, compared to 11 points for the countries that are less globalized. However, policy change was not exclusively or even primarily focused on trade. The list of post-1980 globalizers includes such well-known reformers as Argentina, China, Hungary, India, Malaysia, Mexico, the Philippines, and Thailand, which undertook reforms involving investment liberalization, stabilization, and property rights. The outcome of increased integration into the world economy need not be due to changes in trade policy. [In a World Bank research report D.] Dollar and [P.] Zoido Lobatón find that reliable property rights, strong rule of law, and macroeconomic stability are all associated with more trade and FDI [foreign direct investment]. . . . They also find that it is associated with lower emigration.

As they reformed and integrated with the world market, the "more globalized" developing countries started to grow rapidly, accelerating steadily from 2.9 percent in the 1970s to 5 percent through the 1990s. They found themselves in a virtuous circle of rising growth and rising penetration of world markets. It seems likely that growth and trade reinforced each other, and that the policies of educational expansion, reduced trade barriers, and strategic sectoral reforms reinforced both growth and trade.

The Market Matters

Whether there is a causal connection from opening up trade to faster growth is not the issue. In those low-income countries that have broken into global markets, more restricted access to those markets would be damaging to growth, regardless of whether industrialization was triggered by opening up.

However, opening up integrates an economy into a larger market, and from Adam Smith on economists have suggested that the size of the market matters for growth. A larger market gives access to more ideas, allows for investment in large fixed-cost investments and enables a finer division of labor. A larger market also widens choice. Wider choice for high-income consumers is irrelevant for poverty reduction, but wider choice may have mattered more for firms than for consumers. For example, as India liberalized trade, companies were able to purchase better-quality machine tools. Similar effects have been found for the Chinese import liberalization. Finally, a larger market intensifies competition and this can spur innovation. There is some evidence that integration with the world economy is more important for small and poor economies than it is for large economies like India and China.

There is also a large amount of cross-country regression evidence on openness and growth. This should be treated with caution but not dismissed altogether. [P.] Lindert and [J.] Williamson [of the National Bureau of Economic Research] summarize it:

> The doubts that one can retain about each individual study threaten to block our view of the overall forest of evidence. Even though no one study can establish that openness to trade has unambiguously helped the representative Third World economy, the preponderance of evidence supports this conclusion. One way to see the whole forest more clearly is to consider two sets, one almost empty and one completely empty. The almost-empty set consists of all statistical studies showing that protection has helped Third World economic growth, and liberalization has harmed it. The second, and this time empty, set contains those countries that chose to be less open to trade and factor flows in the 1990s than in the 1960s and rose in the global living-standard ranks at the same time. As far as we can tell, there are no anti-global victories to report for the postwar Third World.

We infer that this is because freer trade stimulates growth in Third World economies today, regardless of its effects before 1940.

To conclude, since 1980 the global integration of markets in merchandise has enabled those developing countries with reasonable locations, policies, institutions, and infrastructure to harness their abundant labor to give themselves a competitive advantage in some manufactures and services. The initial advantage provided by cheap labor has sometimes triggered a virtuous circle of other benefits from trade. For example, when Bangalore [India] initially broke into the world software market, it did so by harnessing its comparative advantage in cheap, educated labor. As more firms gravitated to the city it began to reap economies of agglomeration. The increased export earnings financed more imports, thereby both intensifying competition and widening choice. There is some evidence that between them these four effects of trade raise not only the level of real income, but also its rate of growth. However, the growth process is complex. Trade is certainly not sufficient for growth.

| "Small farmers ... are the immediate and dramatic victims of globalization but the damage is far more widespread."

Globalization Does Not Help Nations Develop

Lila Rajiva

Lila Rajiva is a writer who teaches English and politics at the University of Maryland and Towson University. In the following viewpoint she describes the effects of globalization on her native country of India. She contends that while large multinational corporations offer jobs and economic growth to developing nations, they have a negative impact on the lives of many Third World citizens. For example, such companies often consume excessive amounts of natural resources, such as water, that are needed by local inhabitants. In addition, corporations are attempting to patent indigenous medicines that people have been using freely for centuries.

As you read, consider the following questions:

1. What are the so-called signs of progress on the road from Madras to Vellore, as described by the author?
2. What is hidden behind the rhetoric of the free market, in Rajiva's opinion?

3. How should activists oppose the effects of globalization, in the author's opinion?

The road from Madras to my hometown Vellore in the southern part of India makes for a bumpy ride, regardless of one's choice of transportation—be it a sturdy socialist-era Ambassador car or a newer lightweight import, a crowded dirty bus or an air-conditioned taxi. There are no lanes and the traffic moves erratically and at will, as the black tar fades indistinguishably into the neighboring sand and thorn bushes.

One side of the road has been dug up as part of the preliminary work for the Golden Quadrilateral. Hundred-year-old trees have been cut down to make way for this ambitious national highway that is expected to span the length and breadth of the country. My mother claims that this summer feels a lot hotter thanks to the ceaseless construction. But to what avail this additional three degrees of boiling heat in July when the monsoon fails? Nobody pays attention to the two lanes we have now; why should they care about getting four more?

Signs of "Progress"

Another sign of "progress" along the way is the Hyundai factory. It is one of the many gleaming new buildings—including medical colleges catering to non-resident Indians (Indians who have emigrated outside their country)—dotting the road in this part of the country. Globalization is alive and well in the villages of India.

The meals on the trains used to be served in moistened banana leaves that were plucked in front of you and thrown away after; today they are wrapped in tin foil or come in plastic or cardboard containers like the cheerfully colored juice packs. The Suzuki-owned Marutis [an Indian-made automobile] have been joined by a wide array of foreign makes. I read of high-flying elite and their Porsches and Mercedes Benz—although why anyone would risk taking them out on an Indian road is hard to imagine. I see the plastic knives and forks and cloth napkins in a small town restaurant, internet access in little shops and booths everywhere you go, a small but well stocked air-conditioned supermarket with shopping carts, bored store girls and wide empty aisles.

For a foreign-returned Indian, these symbols of "progress" soothe one's guilt for leaving behind the millions who live an attenuated existence in these paddy fields, huts and impoverished villages. It makes us feel that, finally, the world is getting better thanks to technology and capitalism. The campesino and the conglomerate are working hand in hand as the free market triumphs again.

A Darker Picture

But the gaudy veneer of liberalization is wafer-thin. Lurking beneath is a darker picture, easily visible to anyone who truly wants to see.

Let's take the Hyundai factory as an example. Ever since it opened for business, water has been in short supply for miles around. The locals don't have the water to drink, cook or bathe. In the scorching heat, this shortage is not an inconvenience but a death sentence. [In 2003] the death toll from an unexpectedly hot dry summer reached the thousands.

How does globalization feel when you have to walk a mile to the well with a squalling infant tugging at your sari and nothing to cover your head from the ferocious sun except a thin piece of old cotton? The Hyundai factory guzzles water, electricity and land. But it's good to have something more than the trundling old Ambassadors to drive around. People tell me it's a fine place to work. And won't it be splendid to see the Hyundais zip up and down the Golden Quadrilateral when it's completed.

Jobs, transportation and industry are what globalization brings with it for some, but who stands by to measure the immense fallout borne by everyone else? The collateral damage of multinational companies cannot compete with the devastation inflicted by war. Cancun can't compete with Iraq [where unrest continues after a 2003 war] for the media's attention.[1] But is death from dehydration any less painful than being killed by a bullet?

In the state of Karnataka, small farmers like the campesinos at Cancun have committed ritual suicide to express their outrage at the destruction of their lives by multinationals. They are the immediate and dramatic victims of globalization but the damage is far more widespread if less visible. Some indigenous medicines and herbs used for centuries are now in the danger of becoming the exclusive property of corporations eager to patent them.

A Battle for Intellectual Property Rights

A recent case involved turmeric, the yellow spice used to color rice and other foods in India. In 1995, two expatriate Indians at the University of Mississippi Medical Center, Suman Das and HariHar Cohly, applied for a patent for the use of turmeric as a salve for wounds—an age-old Indian remedy. The Indian Council for Scientific and Industrial Research promptly challenged the patent, even producing an article written in 1953 in the *Journal of the Indian Medical Association* that quoted ancient Sanskrit texts that referred to such use. The patent was eventually withdrawn. But nine other such patents on turmeric have since been filed. Patents have also been granted for specific uses of other indigenous products like basmati rice and neem leaves.

Intellectual property rights are at the core of the World Trade Organization debate between the developed and underdeveloped countries. American trade lawyers argue that since

1. In September 2003 at a World Trade Organization (WTO) meeting in Cancun, Mexico, fourteen thousand farmers and indigenous people from developing nations around the world came to protest conditions they face under the WTO. Kyung Hae Lee, a fifty-six-year-old rice farmer from South Korea, stabbed himself.

patent laws are not frequently used in poorer countries, their governments do not understand them. They claim that only new applications of traditional foods and herbs are being patented, not pre-existing practices. They argue that without patent protection, drug companies have little incentive to undertake long-term and expensive research.

Hidden behind the rhetoric of the free market is a demand for the state to protect the corporation and grant it monopoly rights. And contrary to the rhetoric of the competitive market, it is the biggest companies—such as the pharmaceutical megacorporations with their wealthy executives and fat profit margins—that will profit most from this type of state protection. Meanwhile, millions of children are deprived of the simple vitamins that could save them from disease and death. If the market really worked as it should, freely, the campesinos would win much more frequently than they do now.

A Humane Globalization

But to frame the debate as one between campesino and conglomerate, between the countryside and commerce is to have already lost the war. For capital-G Globalization—like Modernity, Science, Progress, or any other capitalized abstraction—casts itself as irresistible and irreversible. Only Luddites, medievalists, agrarian romantics and the Birkenstock brigade are foolish enough to stand in its way. These are the straw men created by corporate apologists in order to dismiss the anti-globalization movement as irrational or adolescent.

We need new ways of speaking. Modernity is not the enemy. It is the relentless nature of a certain type of economic production, which is propagandized and supported by the state. Without agricultural subsidies, the big farmers would be out of business, beaten out by the small farmers. The conglomerates would be routed by the campesinos.

"Cutting social programs is a good idea, except we don't have any."

Brown. © by Cartoonstock, Ltd. Reproduced by permission.

The resistance to multinationals is not a resistance to globalization. It is a demand to retain the perspective of the village, the perspective of all that is human. What we need today are activists *for* globalization—but a humane globalization, not an inhuman one.

| "Globalization enhances human rights directly by expanding the freedom of people to exercise greater control over their daily lives."

Globalization Increases Human Rights

Daniel T. Griswold

In the following viewpoint Daniel T. Griswold argues that globalization is a form of economic freedom, which in turn leads to political freedom in developing countries. In Griswold's view, open markets provide citizens with more money and the opportunity to buy an assortment of low-cost goods, freeing them from relying upon the vagaries of the state for their needs. Griswold also notes that globalization brings developing nations more technology, allowing the people to communicate with and stay connected to the outside world. Rising incomes and stable lines of communication, he contends, are two factors that commonly lead oppressed populations to demand rights and freedoms. Daniel T. Griswold is the director of the Center for Trade Policy Studies at the Cato Institute, a libertarian public policy research organization.

As you read, consider the following questions:

1. As Griswold explains it, how does the importation of foreign goods free people from some aspects of gov-

ernment tyranny?

2. As the author describes it, what is Michael Novak's Wedge Theory?

3. What percentage of the world's national governments were democratically elected in 2002–2003, according to Griswold?

G lobalization encompasses more than economic efficiency. Expanding trade and investment ties among nations influences the political sphere as well, with implications for human rights and democracy in far corners of the world. Critics of globalization believe that those spillover effects are one more reason for their skepticism.

They argue that the expanding influence of the market undermines political and civil liberties by concentrating power into the hands of a few multinational corporations and by rewarding oppressive governments, such as China's, with lucrative trade deals. But the experience of the last three decades of globalization seems to point in the opposite direction—toward a positive link between economic freedom and political and civil liberties.

Human societies, nation states and civilizations are fantastically complex entities, each with its own history and culture, so it is futile to claim that, for all nations at all times, economic reform and expanding trade will lead quickly to democracy and protection of human rights.

But economists and social scientists have long noted that human freedoms can reinforce each other, and that economic freedom can and often does promote broader human liberties. Nobel-prize economist Milton Friedman, in his book *Capitalism and Freedom,* observed that, "Economic arrangements play a dual role in the promotion of a free society. On the one hand, freedom in economic arrangements is itself a component of freedom broadly understood, so economic freedom is an end in itself. In the second place, economic freedom is also an indispensable means toward the achievement of political freedom."

Free Trade as a Human Right

In that way, globalization enhances human rights directly by expanding the freedom of people to exercise greater control over their daily lives. As barriers to trade, investment, and travel fall, people enjoy more freedom to buy a wider range of quality products at affordable prices because of global competition.

In less developed countries, they no longer need to bribe or beg government officials for permission to import a television set or spare parts for their tractor. Controls on foreign exchange no longer limit their freedom to travel abroad. They enjoy greater freedom to work for foreign-owned affiliates or other private companies rather than for state-owned or government-protected monopolies. As producers, people enjoy more freedom to import machinery and essential inputs to remain in business.

For example, in a closed, state-dominated economy, independent newspapers can easily be deprived of newsprint if they displease the ruling authorities. Union organizers and other workers may hesitate to challenge a government that has the power to turn them out of a job.

Globalization meets the most elementary test of justice, giving to each person sovereign control over that which is his own. As Frederic Bastiat wrote in his 1849 essay, "Protectionism and Communism," "Every citizen who has produced or acquired a product should have the option of applying it immediately to his own use or of transferring it to whoever on the face of the earth agrees to give him in exchange the object of his desires. To deprive him of this option when he has committed no act contrary to public order and good morals,

The Common Thread Between Human Rights and Globalization

The objectives of international human rights and international trade in fact have much in common. Both seek to improve standards of living in larger freedom: one through recognition of what is necessary for a life of dignity—free from fear and want, including access to health care, education, and an adequate standard of living—and the other through the practice of free trade leading to growth, which can then fund vital social programs. The challenge therefore is not to stop the expansion of global markets but to develop institutions and policies—a free and open media, facilities for basic education and health care, economic safety nets, and provisions for women's freedom and rights—that will provide appropriate governance and protect human rights locally, nationally, and at an international level. This will in turn strengthen human development and human security.

Mary Robinson, Peace Review, *March 2004.*

and solely to satisfy the convenience of another citizen, is to legitimize an act of plunder and to violate the law of justice."

Tilling the Soil for Democracy

More broadly, the human contacts, rising incomes, and diffusion of power that come with globalization have created a more hospitable climate for civil and political freedoms around the world. The economic openness of globalization allows citizens greater access to technology and ideas through fax machines, satellite dishes, mobile telephones, Internet access, and face-to-face meetings with people from other countries.

Rising incomes and economic freedom help to nurture a more educated and politically aware middle class. People who are economically free over time want and expect to exercise their political and civil rights as well. In contrast, a government that can seal its citizens off from the rest of the world can more easily control them and deprive them of the resources and information they could use to challenge the authorities.

By creating a more vibrant civil society and economy, globalization nurtures new leaders who can challenge a country's entrenched authority structure. In his book, *Business as a Calling,* social thinker Michael Novak identified this as the Wedge Theory. "Capitalist practices, runs the theory, bring contact with the ideas and practices of the free societies, generate the economic growth that gives political confidence to a rising middle class, and raise up successful business leaders who come to represent a political alternative to military or party leaders. In short, capitalist firms wedge a democratic camel's nose under the authoritarian tent."

The interplay of economic openness and political and civil freedom is admittedly complex, and the question of causation remains unsettled, but the two phenomena are clearly linked in the real world. In the past 30 years, as an expanding share of the world has turned away from centralized economic controls and toward a more open global market, political and civil freedoms have also spread.

The share of the world's population that enjoys full civil and political liberties has risen sharply since 1973, according to Freedom House, the human-rights think tank. Today [in the new millennium] 44 percent of the world's people live in countries Freedom House classifies as "Free," where citizens enjoy the full range of civil and political freedoms, compared to 35 percent in 1973. The share living in countries classified as "Not Free," where those rights are suppressed, has dropped from 47 percent to 35 percent. The share living in countries classified as "Partly Free" has increased slightly from 18 to 21 percent.

As globalization has accelerated since the late 1980s, so too has the global trend toward democracy. Again, according to Freedom House, the share of the world's governments that are democratically elected has spiked up from 40 percent in 1986–87 to 63 percent in 2002–03. Critics of globalization can dismiss the reality of those two powerful trends as a coincidence, but at the very least they undercut the argument that globalization has somehow been bad for democracy.

Open Economies, Free People

As we look more closely at the phenomenon, we see that the dual trends are indeed bound together. When we compare countries according to their record of economic openness and their degree of political and civil freedom, the connection becomes even more evident. People who live in countries that have been relatively open to international trade and investment in the past two decades are far more likely to enjoy full political and civil liberties than those who live in countries that have been relatively closed.

Consider the evidence. *The Economic Freedom of the World: 2001 Annual Report,* a study sponsored by a number of leading think tanks, ranked 93 nations according to the degree of economic openness they maintained from 1980 through 1999. Among the most open countries—those in the top quintile (or 20 percent) of countries ranked according to their economic openness—17 out of 19, or almost 90 percent, are rated "Free" by Freedom House and not a single one is rated "Not Free." The list of those countries that are democratic and also among the most economically open include the United States, Canada, most countries of Western Europe, Taiwan, Australia, New Zealand, and Panama.

In the bottom quintile of openness (i.e. those with the most closed economies), only 2 out of 19, or about 10 percent, are rated "Free" and 7, or more than one-third, are rated "Not Free." The list of countries that have been relatively closed for the past two decades and also lack basic civil and political liberties include Egypt, Pakistan, Algeria, Syria, Iran, Burma, and Burundi. Based on that evidence, countries that maintain a relatively open economy are eight times more likely to be free of political and civil oppression than countries that remain closed. Furthermore, as Milton Friedman noted, an open economy appears to serve as a check against the worst forms of political tyranny.

Recent decades have witnessed dramatic examples of how economic freedom and openness till the soil for civil and political reform. Twenty years ago, South Korea, Taiwan, and Chile were military or one-party dictatorships without free elections or full civil liberties. Today, thanks in large part to economic growth and globalization, all three are thriving democracies where citizens enjoy the full range of civil liberties and where opposition parties have won elections against longtime ruling parties. . . .

Since the end of World War II, the U.S. government's support for trade has been based on the sound assumption that it also promotes democracy and human rights as well as economic development. In an April 2002 speech on the importance of trade promotion authority, President George W. Bush noted that trade is about more than raising incomes. "Trade creates the habits of freedom," the president said, and those habits "begin to create the expectations of democracy and demands for better democratic institutions. Societies that open to commerce across their borders are more open to democracy within their borders. And for those of us who care about values and believe in values—not just American values, but universal values that promote human dignity—trade is a good way to do that."

| "*Globalization ... compromises the capability of the state to ensure the rights of [its] citizens.*"

Globalization Undermines Human Rights

Carlos Castresana Fernandez

Carlos Castresana Fernandez is a visiting professor of law at the University of San Francisco. He served as a public prosecutor in Spain for many years. In the following viewpoint Fernandez claims that globalization has adversely affected human rights. In developing nations, he argues, globalization has stripped governments of their power to safeguard civil liberties and placed citizens at the mercy of multinational corporations. Because the concern for human rights does not keep pace with economic development in these instances, civilian populations end up suffering many social ills such as war, hunger, crime, and corruption as the corporations exploit nations, with no regard for sustained development.

As you read, consider the following questions:

1. How does Fernandez relate Rousseau's "social contract" to his own argument?

2. According to the author, what characterizes the new "wars of globalization?"

3. In Fernandez's view, why are so many developing countries corrupt?

In democratic societies, the state guarantees its citizens the protection of their most fundamental rights for personal development: life, liberty, the right to elect representatives and be elected, equity both of opportunities and justice, as well as many others. These protected rights also bring order to the members of the society in their relations with each other.

Globalization has made possible the access to new communication technologies, has improved transportation and commerce and has also furthered the free movement of persons and goods as well as increased the number of market economies. Globalization has brought numerous advantages to millions but it has also worsened the lives of much of the world's population. The maldistribution of wealth has soared to the levels of the 1920s. As a result, most democratic societies have begun to face great threats to their societies: corruption, political violence and organized crime. These threats are present at all levels of society, and globalization makes it easier for them to germinate.

There are many consequences of these threats. In many non-democratic societies, corruption and violence strengthen authoritarian regimes and prevent political and economic development. In democratic societies, violence and corruption undermine entire social and economic structures and complicate the effective functioning of democratic institutions. In both cases, increased violence and corruption instigate human rights violations. The health of a democratic society is measured by the way it deals with these activities.

The Changing Social Contract

For hundreds of years, international relations were based upon the principle of not interfering in the internal affairs of other states. This meant that the authority of every state renounced

Economic Development Will Not Necessarily Benefit Human Rights

In order to generate significant social and economic change and to focus on the growth and implementation of human rights, countries need to experience economic development, increase in education, particularly for women, and become part of the international communication network. We must also focus on the alleviation of poverty and social inequality, particularly in the "less developed" regions of the world. Countries must develop economic strategies aimed at increasing the basic incomes of individuals and families in the lowest rungs of the socioeconomic ladder. However, wealth or income is only one of the components of poverty. As the 1998 Nobel Laureate in Economics, Amartya Sen, has stated, poverty is a "serious deprivation of certain basic capabilities," such as health care, schooling, and land tenure, among others. Therefore, an increase in a country's GNP [gross national product] will not necessarily result in a reduction in the deprivation of basic necessities. Quite the contrary, . . . we can continue to experience increasing poverty and inequality in the midst of increasing GNP.

Havidán Rodríguez, Social Forces, *September 2004.*

interference with the competences of each other. Sovereignty was articulated on the notion of frontier, which was indispensable in limiting the territory of the sovereign powers. But these geographical frontiers have not been the only mechanisms used to distribute and organize states' power. States have also used structures based on politics, economics, race, culture and religion. But it was the French Revolution that marked the beginning of the generalized use of the concept of human rights to protect citizens against the state. And since then national and international legal instruments have defined human rights and the obligation of the state to prevent the violation of any citizen's rights.

The concept of human rights has always had a revolutionary meaning. The concept of human rights questioned the original ideals of sovereignty because these rights were developed as a mechanism to rectify the previously enforced "natural law" of the strongest controlling the weakest. Human rights were based on the belief that a person is a rational being and therefore the law places everyone at the same level of equality. Sovereignty, in this structure, is passed from the monarchy to the people and from the people to the nation. With time, the people began to choose their representatives through democratic mechanisms. This is the pillar of [philosopher Jean Jacques] Rousseau's "social contract" : the state has the duty to guarantee its citizens the effective enjoyment of their individual rights. Today, this model is subject to alteration because of the progress that has occurred [since the late twentieth century] as well as the violence and corruption that prevent modern states from implementing their duties under the contract. . . .

Globalization has overruled the traditional notion of state sovereignty and compromises the capability of the state to ensure the rights of [its] citizens. The growth of economic powerhouses has increasingly limited the power of governments. Institutions created to protect the rights of sovereign governments have not evolved at the same pace as market economies. The law of the state is being replaced by the law of the market, thus bringing crises that citizens and their representatives have been unable to solve. The invention of the steam engine gave birth to the first industrial revolution, which ignited the world by the end of the nineteenth century. But there is a difference between this technological revolution and the current globalization. While globalization was born out of technology, humanity has now achieved an interconnectedness from which there is no way back.

Poverty and Violence

Social inequalities are but the first of the major effects of globalization. It is not possible for governments and markets to keep planning for the future while ignoring what the majority of the world's population thinks and needs. Between 500 million and one billion people live comfortably but the remaining five billion or more people live in poverty and are subject to war, hunger, disease and underdevelopment. Overpopulation of the planet is seemingly unstoppable, even though hunger kills 30 million people every year in Africa and Asia. . . .

Globalization has also wrought violence and uncontrolled development. The balance between environmental protection and economic development will ultimately be unbearable as the continued exploitation of natural resources generates an unacceptable rate of violence and irreversible environmental deterioration. Citizens of all nations are reverting to the law of the strongest controlling the weakest. But this time there is no monarchy but rather only corporations. . . .

The wars of globalization are wars of attrition and are fought from a distance. Superpowers do not intervene directly, but send and exchange weapons for natural products. The victims of this trade are most often citizens. The Democratic Republic of the Congo (DRC), formerly Zaire, offers a paradigmatic example. The country has suffered more than three-and-a-half million human deaths over the last four years [2000–2004] in a land of great natural resources. The October 2002 report from the UN Security Council states that most of the corporations that buy natural products from the DRC belong to American, Canadian and EU [European Union] member countries, thus breaching the OECD (Organization for Economic Co-operation and Development) rules of transactions with a warring nation. Uganda, one of the countries that border the DRC, participates quite actively in the war, receiving natural resources as payment. The World Bank has pointed out that Uganda's development is based upon the export of minerals that it does not produce.

Corruption

Globalization has further changed the face of corruption. Traditionally, corruption was an individual phenomenon; for example, a public employee earned access to a post and used it for personal gain. Modern corruption . . . affects the effective functioning of democratic systems. This corruption is a generalized corruption, inherent to political and economic systems, that goes beyond individual behavior.

Traditional corruption still affects many countries struggling with development and is often directly linked to ongoing poverty. Nonetheless, many underdeveloped countries are corrupt because developed countries corrupt them. The two are inextricably linked to one another. The corruption index published by Transparency International shows that Bangladesh and Azerbaijan are the two most corrupt countries. But the countries most associated with corrupting countries through bribes are Australia, Sweden and Switzerland. The United States, France and the United Kingdom secure a majority of their international contracts through bribes and political pressure.

Modern corruption is also based on the permanent mingling of the public and private sectors through the trafficking of information; in other words, the use of privileged information for private gain. This is coupled with a constant flow of laundered money from various illegal activities, organized crime, political delinquency and other various forms of corruption that, when combined, will destroy any possibility of equity in economic opportunities.

> "Globalization is not the cause of,
> but a possible partial solution to,
> transnational terrorism."

Globalization Reduces Terrorism

Quan Li and Drew Schaub

Quan Li and Drew Schaub are part of the Department of Political Science at Pennsylvania State University. In the following viewpoint Li and Schaub offer their findings on the connection between transnational terrorism (i.e., terrorism across borders) and economic globalization. While admitting that opening international markets can facilitate the movement of terrorists and their financial capital, the authors suggest that globalization ultimately reduces the risk of terrorism by ameliorating some of its core causes, such as poverty and lack of development.

As you read, consider the following questions:

1. In Li and Schaub's view, how has the digitization of money aided terrorism?

2. According to the authors, what conditions led to the Taliban's takeover of Afghanistan?

3. Through what two "channels" does globalization negatively affect transnational terrorism, in Li and Schaub's opinion?

D o countries that are more integrated into the global economy also experience more transnational terrorist incidents within their borders? In the months following September 11, 2001, many people questioned the future viability of an open global economy, believing that economic globalization had contributed to the transnational terrorist attacks on the World Trade Center and the Pentagon. Indeed, more than $1.4 billion of goods cross the borders of the North American Free Trade Agreement (NAFTA) countries every day. In [2003] alone, cargo vessels off-loaded roughly 18 million 40-foot-long cargo containers at American ports, often in single batches as large as 8,000. Ports and border crossings around the world have similarly experienced an increasing volume of daily shipping and trucking activity. The increasing numbers of trucks and container vessels that facilitate international commerce increase the likelihood of a terrorist successfully smuggling himself or a weapon undetected across a vulnerable border. Financial markets have also experienced a drastic increase in the volume of cross-national transactions. The daily turnover in the foreign exchange market is nearly $2 trillion, exceeding the value of all traded goods and services. The growing number of international financial transactions threatens to overwhelm the enforcement officers who attempt to intercept money meant to sponsor acts of terrorism. Therefore, the risks facing international criminals—including terrorists— who use global networks to facilitate their operations decrease substantially. The global war on terrorism after September 11 has led to tightened security almost around the world, increasing the costs associated with conducting international business.

In contrast, a small number of scholars and policy makers argue that economic openness will result in a reduction in transnational terrorism. Proponents of this view believe that economic globalization promotes economic development, which in turn alters the decision calculus of terrorist groups

---

Globalization and the Path to Stability

Show me where globalization is thick with network connectivity, financial transactions, liberal media flows, and collective security, and I will show you regions featuring stable governments, rising standards of living, and more deaths by suicide than murder. . . . But show me where globalization is thinning or just plain absent, and I will show you regions plagued by politically repressive regimes, widespread poverty and disease, routine mass murder, and—most important—the chronic conflicts that incubate the next generation of global terrorists.

Thomas P.M. Barnett, Esquire, March 2003.

---

toward a reduction in terrorist activities. Progress in economic development due to trade and capital flows removes one of the main incentives for people to engage in terrorist activities out of desperation and poverty. Although this argument is relatively new and less well developed, many policy makers have turned to it for a solution to global terrorism. . . .

Positive Effect of Economic Globalization on Terrorism

Many policy makers, journalists, and scholars believe, especially after the terrorist attacks of September 11, that globalization causes an increase in the frequency of transnational terrorism. . . . Economic globalization can act as a structural constraint that alters the relative costs between legal and illegal activities and affects the decision calculus of transnational terrorists. More specifically, as globalization increases, the cost of illegal activity declines relative to the cost of legal activity, and the overall level of terrorism increases. This decreased risk results from the expansion of the trade, financial, and production investment networks in the global economy.

Computers, chips, and satellites change significantly the structure of international finance, reducing the risks associated with illegal transnational financial transactions. The "digitization" of money allows the wide use of credit cards and smart cards, facilitates the instantaneous transfer of funds across borders, and decreases the probability of being caught in transporting and using illegally obtained funds. . . .

The decreasing effectiveness of governments to monitor financial transactions decreases the risks in the illegal transactions used to sponsor terrorist operations.

Similarly, as the volume of international trade increases, the risk associated with illegal trading also decreases. Trade between the United States, Canada, and Mexico, for example, has more than doubled [since 1994] to at least $1.4 billion worth a day. Over the same period, the number of customs agents responsible for discovering contraband or illegally traded goods has remained the same. Statistics concerning maritime shipments demonstrate the phenomenon even more clearly. Of the 18 million cargo containers that arrive by sea each year in the United States, only 2% to 10% of them are searched. . . .

Transnational terrorists also often take advantage of the international trade network to market goods or services in an effort to marshal resources with which to carry out their criminal activities. Terrorist organizations often rely on the international trade network to trade contraband to fund their various operations. . . .

Negative Effect of Economic Globalization on Terrorism

Advocates of the negative relationship between economic globalization and terrorism claim that economic globalization removes an important cause of transnational terrorism. . . .

A primary cause of transnational terrorism is underdevelopment and poverty, an argument that recently became popular among but was rarely formalized by policy makers and scholars. Poor economic conditions create "terrorist breeding grounds," where disaffected populations turn to transnational terrorist activities as a solution to their problems. In [Palestinian scholar] Marwan Bishara's words, "When people feel so inferior militarily and economically, they adopt asymmetric means—not the usual means—to get what they want." In addition, poverty, underdevelopment, and instability are often associated with those states either willing to provide safe haven for terrorists or unable to successfully expel terrorists from their borders. Poverty and its accompanying instability in Afghanistan created the conditions that allowed the Taliban to gain power, a situation that in turn led to the provision of sanctuary for Al Qaeda and Osama bin Laden. Consistent with this argument, [President George W.] Bush claims in a widely cited speech, "We fight against poverty because hope is an answer to terror." . . .

For economic globalization to reduce transnational terrorism, globalization has to be able to promote economic development and reduce poverty. Many policy makers have endorsed the positive effect of globalization on development. Canadian Finance Minister Paul Martin argues that participation in the global economic system greatly enhances a state's economic development. President Bush also says, "The vast majority of financing for development comes not from aid, but from trade and domestic capital and foreign investment. . . . So, to be serious about fighting poverty, we must be serious about expanding trade." Former U.S. Federal Reserve Board Chairman Alan Greenspan also claims that "the extraordinary changes in global finance on balance have been beneficial in facilitating significant improvements in economic structures and living standards throughout the world." Leaders of the seven major industrial democracies assert in the joint communiqué for the 1996 G7 Summit [a meeting of seven of the top industrialized nations] that "economic growth and progress in today's interdependent world is bound up with the process of globalization." . . .

[Globalization's] negative effect [on terrorism] may be realized through two channels. As a country expands its trade, FDI [foreign direct investment], and financial capital, its growing integration into the global economy arguably improves not only its own economic conditions but also those of its economic partner countries. Economic development in its own national economy removes an incentive for its citizens to engage in transnational terrorist incidents against foreign targets within the country. In addition, economic progress in its major partner countries reduces the likelihood that their citizens will cross borders to this country to engage in terrorist activities. . . .

Globalization Is an Important Aspect of the War on Terror

Based on a sample of 112 countries from 1975 to 1997, we find interesting patterns of statistical association between economic globalization and transnational terrorist incidents. In general, trade, FDI, and portfolio investment of a country do not directly increase the number of transnational terrorist incidents inside its borders. Economic development of the country and its top trading partners reduces the number of terrorist incidents inside the country. To the extent that economic globalization promotes development, globalization can have an indirect negative effect on transnational terrorism.

We should note that our analysis has focused on the linkages between economic globalization and terrorism as a first cut. We raise caution about generalizing the findings to other aspects of the globalization phenomenon. Future research should also look at the effects of immigration, cultural globalization, and the role of transnational nongovernmental organizations if we want to understand fully the effect of globalization on transnational terrorism. . . .

Despite the caveats, our analysis suggests important policy implications for the war against terrorism. National governments should realize that economic globalization is not the cause of, but a possible partial solution to, transnational terrorism. Although opening up one's border facilitates the movement of terrorists and their activities, our results show that the effect of such facilitation appears weak. It does not precipitate a significant rise in transnational terrorist attacks within countries. This is an important lesson for policy makers who are designing antiterrorism policies.

More important, economic openness to the extent that it promotes economic development, may actually help to reduce indirectly the number of transnational terrorist incidents inside a country. Closing borders to foreign goods and capital may produce undesirable effects. Economic closure and autarky can generate more incentives to engage in transnational terrorist activities by hindering economic development. Antiterrorism policy measures should be designed with caution. They should not be designed to slow down economic globalization.

Promoting economic development and reducing poverty should be important components of the global war against terrorism. Such effects are structural and system-wide. It is in the best interest of the United States not only to develop by itself but also to help other countries to grow quickly. The effect of economic development on the number of transnational terrorist incidents is large. The role of economic development deserves much more attention from policy makers than it currently enjoys.

> "Globalisation . . . generates condi-
> tions that are conducive to the
> emergence of extremist movements,
> instability and conflict."

Globalization
Fosters Extremism

Richard Sandbrook and David Romano

In the following viewpoint Richard Sandbrook and David Romano argue that globalization inspires extremism within developing nations. According to the authors, the rapid opening of economic markets is typically a shock to developing countries and commonly involves the destruction of traditional livelihoods as the demand for industrialization takes precedence. Because most developing economies cannot meet the pace of industrialization, chaos ensues, inviting foreign regulation of the new economy, which in turn undercuts the authority of the ruling government and engenders bitterness among the populace. Soon social disparities create protest movements and may foster violence and terrorism. Richard Sandbrook is a member of the Munk Centre for International Studies in Toronto, Canada. David Romano is a postdoctoral scholar at the CÉRIUM international studies center in Montreal, Canada.

As you read, consider the following questions:

Richard Sandbrook and David Romano, "Globalisation, Extremism, and Violence in Poor Countries," *Third World Quarterly,* vol. 25, 2004. Copyright © 2004 by the *Third World Quarterly.* Reproduced by permission of Taylor & Francis, Ltd., www.tandf.co.uk/journals, and the authors.

1. When developing nations face financial crises, what organization commonly steps in to stabilize faltering economies, according to Sandbrook and Romano?

2. In the authors' opinion, in what two ways do growing inequality between the haves and the have-nots breed political turmoil in developing nations under globalization?

3. According to the authors, what are "cultural tool-kits" and how are they used to foster extremism in countries plagued by the injustices of globalization?

That neoliberalism's triumph would usher in a more peaceful and prosperous world—an 'end of history'—was a popular post–cold war view. According to this position, the collapse of state socialism in the 1980s allowed all countries to adopt a market orientation and open economies. Free global markets, it was believed, facilitated the free movement of ideas as well as products, thereby opening closed states to the outside world. Free trade and investment, furthermore, could foster the prosperity necessary to defeat poverty and defuse conflicts. Democratisation and the development of civil societies would, in time, accompany economic liberalism. All these changes would facilitate a more peaceful world.

But a darker view, that liberalisation foments extremist movements and conflict, competed with this sanguine viewpoint. [Karl] Marx had memorably expounded in *The Communist Manifesto* on the volcanic impact of market forces— how they introduce 'everlasting uncertainty and agitation', how 'all that is solid melts into air'—during the first era of globalisation. Similarly, Karl Polanyi in *The Great Transformation* (published in 1944) famously labelled as 'utopian' the liberal project of creating a self-regulating market economy. Such a project invariably instigated a counter-movement of societal protection, for a liberal economy would lead to the 'devastation' of society. However, where the movement towards liberalism and the societal counter-movement entered into deadlock, or where market-induced insecurity became extensive, conditions ripened for the rise of extremist, violent tendencies—fascism and Stalinism in the Europe of the 1920s and 1930s. More prosaically, yet with no less chilling effect, the US Central Intelligence Agency forecast, in its 2000 report *Global Trends, 2015,* that the second era of globalisation would be no less tumultuous than the first:

> [Globalisation's] evolution will be rocky, marked by chronic financial volatility and a widening economic divide. Regions, countries, and groups feeling left behind will face deepening economic stagnation, political instability, and cultural alienation. They will foster political, ethnic, ideological, and religious extremism, along with the violence that often accompanies it.

This darker view frequently surfaces in a neoliberal concern that economic globalisation may provoke a damaging populist backlash against the market economy.

Are the forecasts of Marx, Polanyi and the CIA correct? Our current era is certainly not a peaceful one. Civil wars, insurgencies, ethnic/religious strife, riots, rampant urban crime and terrorism, often abetted by the weakening or collapse of state power, have marred the post–cold war era. Few safe havens exist when even the USA is subjected to a major terrorist attack. Is globalisation implicated in this record of instability and conflict? . . .

We contend that, *as a general tendency,* globalisation—which we take as synonymous with external and internal market liberalisation—generates conditions that are conducive to the emergence of extremist movements, instability and conflict. Virtually the entire human population has been drawn into a growing dependence on markets that, because they are now scantily regulated, subject people to rapid and sometimes devastating changes in fortune. The distributional shifts, new forms of insecurity, and external shocks demand strong, coherent states to take decisive defensive action and mediate domestic conflicts; yet these new tensions, combined with externally influenced austerity programmes and anti-state ideologies, challenge the legitimacy and coherence of already weak states. The rise in tensions and grievances, coupled with an increasingly ineffective and unpopular regime, provide an opening for violent protest movements. Although competition-induced creative destruction may augment global efficiency, this goal is often achieved at the immediate cost of greater uncertainty and upheaval. . . .

With the ascendancy of neoliberalism in the early 1980s, 'structural adjustment' became the principal economic policy imperative in indebted countries. Hitherto, most of these countries had pursued state-led development, featuring import substitution, subsidies, regulation of markets, and varying degrees of state ownership of productive assets. In the 1980s or earlier, these statist economies faltered, especially in Latin America and sub-Saharan Africa. These economic crises derived from multiple sources: exogenous shocks (world recession, interest-rate hikes, energy price increases) and domestic constraints (neopatrimonial politics, corruption, mismanagement, armed conflicts, instability). Something needed to be done. The neoliberal prescription involved a rapid shift from state-led to market-led development. To compete in global markets and attract capital, the new model enjoined governments to maintain low inflation, reduce production costs, cut corporate taxes and labour costs, limit subsidies, privatise land and public corporations, and liberalise markets. These changes, whatever their economic merits, have had profound social and political implications. . . .

Traditional Economies Destroyed

In agriculture neoliberal policy typically prescribes a reduction or elimination of price controls and subsidies to producers, in addition to export orientation and low tariffs, as the best way to improve economic conditions. Such a programme can wreak havoc with the livelihoods of smallholders, as the case of India shows. India liberalised ... soy bean and soy oil imports in August 1999. The result was that subsidised imports from Western countries rose by 60% in the first year. [According to A. Mittal in an International Forum on Globalization special report,] 'Prices crashed by more than two-thirds, and millions of oilseed-producing farmers had lost their market, unable even to recover what they had spent on cultivation. The entire edible oil production and processing industry was also destroyed. Millions of small mills have closed down.' The phasing out of fertiliser subsidies—often required under IMF [International Monetary Fund] conditionality—raises production costs, and helps drive many small farmers into insolvency.

As policies such as these drive many smallholders to the wall, export-orientated large companies buy them out. Former farmers head for the burgeoning urban slums. Export receipts may increase and subsidised wheat and rice imports from the EU [European Union] and the USA may lower food prices, but at the expense of declining food self-sufficiency, growing insecurity and inequality, and much bitterness.

Trade liberalisation in industry also produces many losers, along with winners. Even if the freer trade maintains or increases overall output and labour productivity, it will lead to the failure of some firms, to widespread retrenchment of workers, and to unemployment in some sectors. Chronic insecurity grows, especially in industrialised countries like the USA, where unions are weak, as industries rapidly wax and wane, better-paid permanent jobs vanish, and unskilled and even skilled workers watch their real wages fall. That this insecurity fosters anger, intolerance, and extremism should not be surprising.

Financial Crises

This policy shift breeds periodic currency crises that undercut living standards and employment. Liberalisation of domestic banking, followed by international financial deregulation, has opened up cross-border capital movements throughout the world since the 1980s. IMF conditionality presses developing countries in the direction of removing capital controls. Today, at least $1.5 trillion passes through currency markets each day in a world of instantaneous trading where markets never close. The result is a high volatility of financial flows leading to 'turbulence': a rise in the frequency and severity of financial crises. Mexico in 1994, Thailand, Indonesia, South Korea and Russia in 1997–98, Brazil in 1999, and Turkey and Argentina in 2000–03 are just the most recent instances of devastating financial crises resulting in a collapse in the local currency, in economic activity and in employment. One expert estimates that these crises raised the incidence of poverty by 7% in these eight countries—pushing an extra 57 million people below the poverty line. Financial liberalisation, therefore, is a major contributor to the chronic insecurity of the market system.

IMF-style stabilisation programmes, designed to remedy financial disequilibria, can raise societal tensions and thereby foster conflict. The standard package includes exchange-rate devaluation, positive real interest rates, a sharp decline in money supply, and a cut in governmental expenditures. But slashing public spending will usually result in a reduction or elimination of popular subsidies, job losses, wage cuts, and a reduction of public investment and services. The net result may be to sabotage implicit social contracts, the tacit bargains whereby sectors of the population assent to rule in exchange for the public provision of customary services and material benefits. . . .

Growing Inequality

Domestic and external liberalisation has also deepened certain inequalities within societies. Since the early 1980s, 'inequality has risen in most countries, and in many cases sharply' [according to G.A. Cornia and J. Court in *Inequality, Growth and*

The Militarization of Globalization

The war on terror has resulted in the militarisation of globalisation, according to which the integration of markets
remains the main economic imperative, but is pursued
within the framework of the global security agenda. The
militarisation of globalisation effectively allows the global
powers to bring military force to bear in securing their
economic interests, removing opposition and threats and,
with them, people's economic, social, cultural and political
rights. Such political repression and military suppression
mainly affect the poorest and most marginalised sectors
and communities. As a result, political and social conditions that foster exclusion, poverty and underdevelopment
are exacerbated. Weaker sectors of the domestic economy,
often the means of livelihood of the poorest groups in society, are the most vulnerable to the negative impacts of
military operations.

*Antonio Tujan, Audrey Gaughran, and
Howard Mollett,* Race & Class, *vol. 46, 2004.*

Poverty in the Era of Liberalisation and Globalisation]. A de-
tailed study of 73 countries for which high-quality data were
available revealed that inequality rose in 48 cases (accounting
for 59% of the sample's population), remained constant in 16
countries (although inequality rose in two of them, Indonesia
and Bangladesh, in the late 1990s), and fell in only nine countries, accounting for 5% of the total population. Other studies
confirm this general trend. Although data are limited, they
also point to the growth of regional inequality. China, India
and Thailand manifest growing regional gaps and high rates
of rural-urban migration. Growing regional disparities may
exacerbate ethnic cleavages, as ethnic groups are generally re-
gionally based.

This worsening income distribution is directly related to neoliberal policies. Economic stabilisation programmes induce deep recessions while cutting expenditures that benefit the poor (food subsidies, public employment, accessible education and health care). Financial liberalisation, besides inducing periodic recessions, shifts income to lenders and renters at the expense of wages and borrowers. Privatisation often concentrates the ownership of public assets in the hands of wealthy political insiders, further exacerbating inequality. Tax systems tend to become less progressive and more reliant on value-added taxes, less redistributive and more reliant on user payments, all of which promotes inequality. And the quest for more 'flexible' labour markets generally translates into reduced employment protection, lower minimum wages, curtailed union rights and falling public employment. In all these ways liberalisation and globalisation hammer the living standards and prospects of middle-class sectors and workers in many countries, while benefiting the owners of capital—physical, financial and intellectual.

Growing inequality breeds political turmoil in two ways. First, rising inequality reduces the contribution that economic growth (where achieved) makes to reducing poverty. Defined as those who survive on less than $1 per day (1985 purchasing power parity), the very poor remained constant at about 1.2 billion people between 1987 and 1998, according to the World Bank. By the latter date, nearly half the world's population still lived below the higher poverty line of $2 per day. Expectations that free markets would transform the living standards of the poor have, therefore, been dashed in many countries, with potentially disruptive effects. Second, relative deprivation is a more powerful motivator of inter-group violence than absolute deprivation. A large-scale quantitative study [conducted by E.W. Nafziger and J. Auvinen in 2002] concludes: 'The risk of political disintegration increases with a surge of income disparities by class, region and community'.

This political disintegration can take two forms. On the one hand, in highly stratified class societies, growing inequality will deepen class conflict and often augment the appeal of left-wing movements. This pattern has characterised much of Latin America. Particularly explosive are the likely social consequences of the liberalisation of agricultural markets and the creation of private property in land where smallholders had hitherto held communal rights to land use. The increased vulnerability and insecurity of rural populations have fomented conflicts along class or ethnic lines. On the other hand, in countries where deep communal cleavages have emerged since independence (as in parts of Africa and Asia), growing disparities have exacerbated regional, ethnic and/or religious divisions. . . .

Undermining State Control

Whether these tensions will afflict a particular country and foster conflict and instability depends heavily on the capacity of its state to mediate and disarm them. Yet neoliberalism can weaken the capacity of states to maintain order. If states had begun to disintegrate before the initiation of stabilisation and liberalisation, the latter processes undercut them further. Two tendencies undermine state effectiveness. First, the legitimacy and mediatory capacity of a state depends heavily on its provision of basic services—education, health, clean water, roads—together with its mounting of safety nets and its servicing of extensive patron-client networks. However, external shocks (reduction of aid, declines in the terms of trade, outflows of foreign capital), IMF-sponsored stabilisation programmes and privatisation of state corporations will curtail a government's resources just as societal tensions rise. Central governments will then be less able to manage conflict by compensating the regions, classes and unemployed who bear the brunt of the adjustments; indeed, they may be unable even to maintain order, as emboldened rebels defy central authority.

The latter may capture lucrative local resources—gold, diamonds, oil or timber—in order to build their own patronage networks. Second, the authority of the government will suffer if it is seen as the puppet of external forces, such as the IMF or the US government. . . .

Market liberalisation, therefore, not only heightens the insecurity and uncertainty of certain groups in characteristic ways, but also may deepen existing social cleavages (and create new ones) by widening the gap between winners and losers while circumscribing a state's capacity to deliver valued services and patronage. The demographic trends tend to magnify the potential for political unrest. In many developing countries, half of the rapidly expanding population is under 25 years of age. Young men without prospects—the contemporary embodiment of Marx's 'dangerous classes'—are disproportionately represented among those adversely affected by market conditions.

Cultural Responses to Injustice

Yet rebellion and violence are not the necessary outcome of these stresses on the social fabric. An adept regime strategy either to buffer the losers' living standards, enhance equity and build a new political base or, alternatively or concomitantly, to repress the dissidents, may quell the turbulence. Alternatively, the rise in insecurity and sense of inequity, if coupled with an increasingly ineffective and unpopular regime, provides openings for extremist movements and political violence. The domestic political consequences of transnational strains depend heavily on the depth of pre-existing cleavages, the organisation and goals of dissident groups, and the flexibility and coherence of institutions.

Protest movements try to translate inchoate grievances into a sense of injustice and threat, and thereby to mobilise people for political action. Counter-elites manipulate 'cultural tool-kits'—dominant symbols, myths, historical memories, and attitudes—to interpret events, attribute blame and sanction action, including political violence. Leaders compete to 'frame' issues in a way that will gain support among their target audience. The ideological content of these radical movements ranges from the far left to the far right. In Chiapas in southern Mexico, for instance, peasants have responded to a compatible blend of liberation theology and Marxism, together with the imagery of Emilio Zapata, in rallying behind the EZLN (Zapatistas) since the mid-1980s. 'Globalizing economic, political and cultural forces merged with the impact of historically derived conditions and the activism of mobilizers, tying local realities ... to wider world currents', observes one analyst of the Chiapas rebellion.

Similarly, Islamism, whose upsurge in popular support coincides with the current era of globalisation, has become the main ideology of protest in predominantly Islamic countries. Islamism offers a 'religio-historical justification' for revolt in a context where other protest ideologies—populism, nationalism, socialism and pan-Arabism—have failed to achieve their anti-imperialist, nationalist, egalitarian goals. Islamists provide basic services in poor areas, champion the Islamic heritage in opposition to alien cultural influences, crystallise feelings of discontent and deprivation (especially among the young), condemn corrupt and authoritarian regimes, and articulate the anger aroused by the Israeli-Palestinian conflict. Grievances arising from economic trends and persistent poverty thus blend with cultural and geopolitical tensions to fortify Islamist support.

By identifying the machinations of specific groups (defined by class, ethnicity, nation or religion) as directly responsible for detrimental trends, radical movements focus popular frustration and anger. Therein lies the rationale for political violence, for how else can the powerful manipulators be defeated and the proper order restored?

Periodical Bibliography

The following articles have been selected to supplement the diverse views presented in this chapter.

Nancy Birdsall, Dani Rodrik, and Arvind Subramanian	"How to Help Poor Countries," *Foreign Affairs*, July/August 2005.
David Dollar	"Globalization and Poor Nations: Opportunities and Risks," *Phi Kappa Phi Forum*, Fall 2003.
Rodger Doyle	"Winners and Losers," *Scientific American*, July 2003.
Luiz Fernando Furlan	"Why We All Need Fair Trade," *Global Agenda*, January 2004.
Barbara Gunnell	"A Conspiracy of the Rich," *New Statesman*, May 24, 2004.
Doug Henwood	"Beyond Globophobia," *Nation*, December 1, 2003.
Kema Irogbe	"Globalization and the Development of Underdevelopment of the Third World," *Journal of Third World Studies*, Spring 2005.
John Kampfner	"Terrorism: The Price We Pay for Poverty," *New Statesman*, February 3, 2003.
Peter Marber	"Globalization and Its Contents," *World Policy Journal*, Winter 2004/2005.
Andres Mejia-Vergnaud	"Effects of Globalization," *Society*, March/April 2004.
Cait Murphy	"The Hunt for Globalization That Works," *Fortune*, October 28, 2002.
Klaus Schwab	"Building the Future," *Newsweek*, December 17, 2001.

What Is the State of Democracy in the Third World?

Chapter Preface

In the 1970s, when the most recent wave of democracy began to spread across the globe, only 25 percent of nations had democratically elected governments. By the beginning of the new millennium, however, democracy had become the most prevalent form of governance. Pushed by the fall of Soviet communism and the power of globalization, about 75 percent of the world's countries held participatory elections of one kind or another. In the Third World, the move toward democracy has been dramatic. For example, every Latin American government (with the exception of Cuba) has been popularly elected, and in Asia and Africa, only a few governments hold on to authoritarian control.

Some caution that the legacy of regional despots has scarred developing nations, leaving the new democracies either teetering on the edge of sustainability or undermined by entrenched bureaucracies that still really hold the power. A few even point to pseudo-democracies such as Malaysia and Singapore, which have tried to marry democratic institutions to single-party governments. In addition, many outright dictatorships remain—especially in sub-Saharan Africa—in stark contrast to neighboring governments experimenting with democratic change. And some developing nations insist that strong central government, not a multiparty electorate, is needed to keep focused on economic growth.

The champions of democracy, however, argue that any progress toward democracy benefits the overall development of Third World nations. In a 2001 article for the *Harvard International Review*, student scholar Yu-Ping Chan maintains that "an open political system helps root out pervasive corruption, which hurts development and discredits public authority. With democracy, a government has to account for its policies before an ever-demanding public, thus ensuring greater transparency and reining in corruption." Advocates such as Chan insist that democracy, once having taken hold in Third World countries, is difficult to thwart. Even in imperfect democracies, the taste of civil liberties creates a desire for greater freedom, compelling citizens to agitate for improvement.

It is likely, then, that the impact of democracy in the Third World as a whole is indeterminate. As well-known scholars such as politics professors Jeffrey Haynes and Robert Pinkney have separately concluded, democracy in the developing world is a comparatively recent phenomenon. Few elected governments have had the time, resources, or political clout to effect lasting change. Although a scant number of democratic Third World countries—most notably, Pakistan—have reverted back to authoritarian government, most still progress toward openness and freedom while struggling with issues of economic growth, civil liberties, ethnic strife, and multiparty politics.

> "*Democratic . . . governments have been sprouting up across the continent since the end of the Cold War.*"

Democracy Is Succeeding in Africa

Howard W. French

Howard W. French is the Shanghai, China, bureau chief of the New York Times. In the following viewpoint French argues that many African governments are making great strides toward democracy and accountability to their citizens. Using Mali as an example, French comments on how some Africa nations are shucking off their despotic pasts and building vibrant, responsible governments that are improving health care, public services, and education. French also attests, however, that much of these positive efforts are going unnoticed by the United States, which has written off Africa as strategically worthless and lacking the potential for betterment.

As you read, consider the following questions:

1. According to French, what topics concerning Africa are making headlines in the United States, and how are these stories affecting U.S. perceptions of that continent?

2. In French's view, what accounts for the failure of de-

Howard W. French, "The Hope of Africa, Beyond War and Disaster There Is Plenty," *Crisis*, vol. 111, November/December 2004. Copyright © 2004 by the Crisis Publishing Company, Inc. Reproduced by permission of the publisher and the author.

mocracies in some African countries?

3. What problem in the United States does French say accounts for America's stinginess toward Africa?

E very one of us knows Africa through its tragedies.

Even those who cannot name more than a handful of the continent's capitals, just like those who ignore the broad outlines of its rich history, become aware of Africa intermittently through its wars, its coups, its famines and its other humanitarian disasters.

Today [in late 2004], it is Sudan, which has emerged from this anonymity through the power of the news. As you read this, Western governments continue a sterile debate over the meaning of genocide, or whether or not the term even applies in Sudan—a land vaster than the entire continental United States east of the Mississippi River. Meanwhile, tens of thousands of people are being displaced at gunpoint and driven into refugee camps, and innocent men, women and children are dying in untold numbers.

Only yesterday, it seems, we learned through the ephemera of headlines that in the Democratic Republic of the Congo, another vast African nation, more than 3 million people died in a series of conflicts unleashed by the war in 1997 to overthrow Mobutu Sese Seko, a longtime partner of the U.S. government.

If such horrible figures are to be believed, this latest Congo crisis, with its echoes of the crisis that attended the country's rise to independence from Belgian colonial rule in 1960, ranks as the most costly conflict in human lives anywhere on earth since World War II.

Yet how many of us made it past the headlines and paused to focus our thoughts on the consequences for African Americans, indeed for humanity, of chaos and bloodshed on such a scale? Judging from countless conversations I've had about Africa over the years, I would wager that many among the small number who did, threw up their hands in despair over Africa and concluded the continent is a lost cause.

Ignoring Real Progress

Earlier this year [2004] I published a book entitled *A Continent for the Taking: The Tragedy and Hope of Africa,* and in touring the United States to talk about Africa, found myself running into exactly this sort of question with remarkable frequency. Indeed, even many people who had read the book told me that they came away much more convinced of the tragedy, rather than the hope, of my subtitle.

As tempting as it can be to give in to pessimism over Africa, however, I strongly believe that to do so is simply wrong. Doomsayers, and they are not in short supply these days, make two fundamental mistakes when looking at Africa. The first error is assuming that Africa, the world's second-largest continent, three times larger than the United States, and home to more than 700 million people, is incapable of change or that its problems are beyond the help of the outside world. The second mistake, and it is a related one, is focusing on Africa's tragedies while ignoring the continent's very real progress toward democratic governance, a development that holds the key to reducing poverty and turmoil on the continent.

They further compound these errors by overlooking one of Africa's greatest potential assets: its ancestral and historic ties to the United States. African Americans are for Africa, a vital but unrealized constituency, one whose voice could and should affect the way the United States engages the continent.

The Promise of Democracy

Those who see little hope in Africa make far too little, I believe, of one of the most important developments in the world in the post–Cold War period: the spreading of democratic government across the African continent. Because our news media is by nature pessimistic, the phenomenon of African democracy competes poorly with a story line built around disaster, even though its longer-term significance is arguably far greater.

In *A Continent for the Taking,* I devoted two chapters to one African country whose flourishing democracy inspired me greatly: Mali. This landlocked West African state, which sits astride a huge, arid belt known as the Sahel, located to the immediate south of the Sahara Desert, is poor and largely bereft of natural resources. Yet in the face of manifold material and natural handicaps, the Malian people peacefully overthrew a long-time military dictatorship and established a democracy in 1992. Democratic governance has dramatically changed the way of life of an entire nation after more than 30 years of independent misrule and many more decades of colonial misgovernment by France before the country gained independence in 1960.

Today, instead of public funds being raked off and banked in numbered accounts in Switzerland for the benefit of a small clutch of leaders, Mali's finances are being managed in a transparent fashion. This allows the state to use its meager resources for the purposes of development: building roads, healthcare clinics and schools, and seeing to it for the first time that girls are educated in large numbers.

Any quick consultation of modern political science textbooks would suggest that what happened in Mali should have never occurred. For democracy to arise, a country is first supposed to be relatively prosperous, with a significant middle-class, high rates of literacy and a rich tradition of civic activism. Mali had none of these things, and yet there it has been, [since 1992], regularly electing public officials in and out of office from the presidency on down.

Not an Isolated Case

Mali's achievement would be merely a pleasant curiosity if it were an isolated case. Fortunately, for Africa, though, its example stands out less and less each year.

Flawed Democracy Is Still Progress

Africa's much-publicized failures obscure the evolving political landscape after a decade when millions of first-time voters cast ballots from the deserts of Mali to the green hills of South Africa.

South Africa, Mozambique and Senegal are among those countries taking steps forward, even as others falter. . . .

In May [2002], thousands of jubilant voters in Sierra Leone cast ballots for president in the country's first elections since its civil war, which lasted throughout the 1990's. In Lesotho, which was battered by an attempted coup in 1998, citizens peacefully elected a new Parliament that same month.

With the longstanding leaders of Mozambique, Namibia and Angola announcing that they will not run for re-election, more political transitions seem likely.

Rachel L. Swarns, with Norimitsu Onishi,
New York Times, *June 2, 2002*

Democratic and increasingly accountable governments have been sprouting up across the continent since the end of the Cold War. To be sure, several African countries, including Zambia, Malawi, Niger, Gambia and even war-torn states like Angola, Congo-Brazzaville, Sierra Leone and Liberia, have experimented with democratic governance, only to suffer setbacks. Their failures may be laid to bad leadership, ethnic division and a generalized lack of support from the outside world. The point of overriding importance, however, is that overall, the community of democratic states in Africa remains on the rise. The ranks of these countries include a mixture of old democratic stalwarts like Botswana and Mauritius, and more recent additions like South Africa, Benin, Ghana, Senegal, Tanzania, Mozambique, Lesotho and Kenya. Even Nigeria, Africa's most populous nation, with more than 100 million citizens, has had democratic rule since the late 1990s, albeit a rougher approximation of the ideal.

To be sure, there are other reasons to be encouraged about Africa's future, from the peaceful end of apartheid in South Africa, to the end of long, post-colonial wars in countries like Angola and Mozambique, and even a peace settlement between the Sudanese government and rebels in the south, who had been fighting for two decades. There have also been extraordinary successes in the fight against AIDS in Uganda, once the world leader in infection rates, at roughly 30 percent. By 2003, through a determined public health effort, that rate had declined to 7 percent.

The preeminent importance of democracy to the continent, however, was made clear in an issue of *Foreign Affairs,* a leading policy journal. According to the magazine, people living in low-income democracies live, on average, nine years longer than their counterparts in autocracies. Their children have a 40 percent greater chance of attending secondary school. They benefit from agricultural yields that are 25 percent higher, on average, and have 20 percent fewer infant deaths. Low-income democracies score between 15 to 25 percent stronger on indices of corruption and rule of law than autocracies. Perhaps most importantly, the study found, countries undergoing democratic reform experience armed conflict half as often as the norm in sub-Saharan Africa.

Fortunately, the movement toward democracy in Africa has achieved enough momentum so that the African Union, Africa's one continent-wide organization, pushed through the creation of a mechanism of potentially dramatic historic significance: a peer review system of African governments to inhibit corruption and foster good governance. Encouragingly, 16 African governments have signed up so far. . . .

Alone in the World

Rather than being surprised at African misgovernment, one should be permitted to marvel that things have not turned out even worse. As Americans, we can be truly proud of the transformative role our country has so often played in the world, and never more than in the last six decades. During that time, we lifted Europe out of the widespread devastation in the aftermath of the Second World War. We helped Japan create a modern economy and jump-started South Korea, putting it on a fast track to growth in the wake of the Korean War. Latin America has seen a similar infusion of American technology and capital.

When we look at the world in this light, we are forced to realize that only Africa has been left out of the party. Only Africa has failed to benefit from American largesse in the form of aid—the United States is among the most miserly donors of aid, on a per capita basis, of all of the major industrialized nations. And, perhaps even more crucially, has failed to benefit from the irrigation in capital and human capacity that come from the kind of broad relationship with the United States that we have seen our country develop with every other part of the world.

Why has Africa been left out in the cold? It is because we have been told that the continent holds no strategic interest for the United States. It is because rather than embracing the continent as a promising and lucrative new frontier for investment, we have been told, in the words of former U.S. Senator Jesse Helms, that Africa is a "rat hole" into which we throw vast sums of aid money only to see it disappear.

Manifestly, the strategic and economic arguments against greater involvement do not survive close examination. Fully 13 percent of the American population can trace its ancestry, at least in part, to Africa.

As long as a decade ago, each major region of Africa boasted as much trade with the United States as all of the constituents of the former Soviet Union combined. Today, the continent is the source of about 18 percent of the United States's oil imports, and this figure is set to rise sharply over the next couple of decades, perhaps rising as high as 25 percent. With our nation engaged in war in the Middle East, no one needs to be reminded there are few products in today's world more strategic than oil.

Still, it would be a serious mistake to limit our attention to Africa to the development of the petroleum industry. It is yet another extractive business, much like the mining for diamonds, gold, uranium, copper and cobalt that have received large Western investments but which, by their very capital-intensive nature, have done little to further local development.

Discrimination Against Africans

Why mince words?

I am convinced that Africa's isolation, and our stinginess toward the continent is related to the very same long-term discrimination and disdain that Americans of African descent have battled against from our earliest days on this continent. One of the most costly and insidious results of the transatlantic slave trade was the near-total disconnect between Africans and African Americans, which continues to this day.

Blacks in the United States are by far the wealthiest and potentially most powerful people of African ancestry anywhere in the world, yet the experience of slavery and our subsequent history in this country has severely damaged our links of kinship, language and culture with the continent of our origin. Malcolm X, speaking before the Organization of African Unity, in 1964, put his finger on the problem when he told the continent's leaders: You will not be respected until and unless African Americans are respected. And African Americans will not be respected until Africans are respected. . . .

Tremendous hope for Africa, and for African Americans, lies in the benefits for all to be obtained by unlocking the potential Black America represents as a constituency. Once that is done, no future American president would imagine saying, as our leaders have said in the past, that Africa holds no strategic interest for the United States.

| "The struggle for democracy in many
parts of Africa will remain on hold."

Democracy Faces Major Obstacles in Africa

Ike Oguine

In the following viewpoint Ike Oguine, a writer living in Lagos, Nigeria, asserts that many African nations are fighting to safeguard their democratic governments from the interests of autocratic presidents. As Oguine notes, several countries have successfully fended off corrupt and abusive tyrants clinging to power, but in other parts of developing Africa, the story is bleaker. In nations such as Somalia and Togo, autocrats have remained in power, eliminating the opposition and oppressing the citizenry. Until these despots are deposed, Oguine states, democracy cannot spread.

As you read, consider the following questions:

1. Why does Oguine say that the successful defeat of President Muluzi's amendment to the Malawi constitution may not signal that the political battle is over?

2. Why were NGOs "ringing alarm bells" in Sierra Leone, according to Oguine?

3. As the author reports, whose bodies washed up on the shores of Benin in 1998?

Ike Oguine, "A Narrow Victory," *New Internationalist*, vol. 351, November 2002.

T he Malawian Parliament, by only three votes, defeated an attempt by President Bakili Muluzi to change the country's constitution [in 2002]. The change would have allowed Muluzi to run for a third term in office. Many Africans far beyond Malawi's borders were jubilant. Letters poured into the Africa Service of the BBC [British Broadcasting Corporation], ironically one of the liveliest pan-African forums around, congratulating Malawians for successfully resisting the return of the Life-President Syndrome that has so terribly scarred Africa.

Many opposition politicians had agreed to vote for the amendment sought by Muluzi's party. With their votes it had seemed that the President would have no difficulty in getting rid of the constitutional restriction on his running for a third term. However, a broad coalition of forces, including former cabinet ministers, churches and non-governmental organizations (NGOs), mounted a determined campaign against the amendment and managed to win enough parliamentary support to defeat it. Though the battle is by no means over, as Muluzi's supporters say they will try again, the victory won at least so far by Malawian pro-democracy forces is indeed significant. It is yet another indication that the democratic coalitions which in the 1990s ended decades of autocratic rule in many African countries will do everything they can to protect their hard-won gains. These democratic forces recognize that the struggle does not end when the autocrat is forced to give up power: it only enters a new phase.

Guarding Democracy from Autocrats

From fighting bare-knuckled dictatorship (and in many cases making incredible sacrifices), the struggle has shifted to guarding the new processes of democracy from the rampaging ambitions of political leaders. In Zambia, a coalition similar to Malawi's was successful in preventing President Chiluba from changing the constitution to allow him to run a third term

Zimbabwe's Failed Progress Toward Democracy

Zimbabwe's elections at the end of March 2005 anchored the negative end of the spectrum [of African nations adhering to supposed democratic elections] during the past year. Although the balloting was less overtly violent than at other times in the country's history, President Robert Mugabe sought to hold on to power by various means. He gained the right to appoint people of his choice to fill 30 of the 150 seats in the parliament. The government designed electoral boundaries to generate more safe seats for the ruling party. In the two years prior to the election it arrested opposition leaders on several occasions and introduced a bill to ban human rights groups and other NGOs that received any foreign funding. Youth groups attached to the ruling party engaged in political harassment, and there were reports of threats to deny food to those who voted against Mugabe. Journalists worked under increasingly tight restrictions after the 2002 Access to Information and Protection of Privacy Act gave the minister of information broad powers to confer or deny licenses for reporters and publications. When the elections were held, an estimated 10 percent of registered voters were turned away without being able to cast ballots.

Jennifer Widner, Current History, *May 2005.*

in office. Across Africa there are many other examples of groups in recently redemocratized countries which are not just trying to protect democratic institutions but striving to make them more participatory and responsive. Even as the world was praising Sierra Leone's relatively free and fair elections that followed years of savage civil war, for example, NGOs in the country were ringing alarm bells. What the outside world saw as a move towards democracy, Sierra Leonian democratic activists saw as a potential return to the past, where two insensitive and corrupt political parties held sway. They feared a return to mass discontent, widespread bitterness and civil conflict.

Nigeria's NLC and South Africa's COSATU are further examples: rank-and-file trade-union groups resisting in their countries the application of one-size-fits-all economic policies fashioned in Washington.

Enforcing constitutional term limits, seeking to broaden democratic participation and challenging market fundamentals are all important in themselves. But it is perhaps even more important that these various struggles are revitalizing democratic debate in societies which have been under repressive rule for a very long time. They are ensuring that our news democracies do not lapse into complacency, do not become nice curtains to be displayed to the world while power élites continue to transact business as usual among themselves.

Democracy on Hold

Of course there are still too many countries in Africa where the journey away from autocracy has not even begun. The [New Internationalist], in its August [2002] edition, reported that out of 53 nations in Africa only 21 are electoral democracies. The rest range from Somalia, which for many years has remained a 'failed state' paralyzed by inter-clan conflict, to Egypt which has a national parliament of sorts but where a system of secretive military courts hands out summary (in)justice to opponents of the Government. Recent peace agreements in the Democratic Republic of Congo and Sudan hold out some hope that the wars in those countries may be brought to an end soon. However, if the fate of past agreements is anything to go by, any such hope must be cautious indeed. And until these and other bitter civil wars can be brought to an end, the struggle for democracy in many parts of Africa will remain on hold.

With a combination of savage brutality and extreme wiliness, our longest surviving autocrat, Togo's President Eyadema, has frustrated years of struggle to hold free and fair elections in his country. In 1998, independent civil-rights groups reported that the bodies of several of his political opponents had washed up along Togo's beautiful beaches and in neighboring Benin—killed by Eyadema's security forces for protesting against fraudulent elections he'd organized. Not long after that France's President [Jacques] Chirac paid a visit to Eyadema and large posters of the two ageing politicos beaming at each other dotted the streets of Lomé, Togo's capital. Even a brutalized people could not help but seethe in anger.

So it is certain that several grim battles lie ahead in the struggle for democracy in Africa. Heavy sacrifices will continue to be required of people who have already given so much while a cynical or largely inattentive world offers at best formulaic noises. Nevertheless, the message from Malawi is a positive one; when the autocrat is finally defeated, a façade of electoral democracy to satisfy the formal requirements of aid donors will not be acceptable, neither will regression to 'constitutional autocracy.' Africa's democrats want the real thing— and will fight very hard for it.

| *"Latin Americans can't seem to make democracy work."*

Democracy Is Failing in Latin America

William Ratliff

William Ratliff is a fellow and curator of the Americas Collection at the Hoover Institution. In the following viewpoint Ratliff states that democracy is not taking hold in Latin America. In Ratliff's view, several nations have aspirations toward democratic rule, but self-serving leaders who are still managing the vestiges of oppressive colonial governments have no incentive to relinquish control. In order to bring about democracy, Latin Americans will have to work to undo the apparatus of state control left over from colonial days.

As you read, consider the following questions:

1. What does Ratliff mean when he says policy makers in Washington concentrate too "narrowly on a few yardsticks like periodic votes and trade agreements?"

2. What examples of social and political instability in Latin American history does the author cite?

3. What does Alvaro Varga Llosa, as quoted by the author, mean when he says, "Reform ultimately involves undoing more than doing?"

L atin Americans can't seem to make democracy work. Ec-uador now [in 2005] has its seventh president in nine years. [In 2005] Bolivian Indians overthrew their second president in less than two years. In 2001 the majority Indian population in Peru elected one of its own as president, after his predecessor had fled the country, but as *The Economist* of London reported . . . he has long been the region's most unpopular president.

And that's just the beginning. The decades-long guerrilla/ drug war in Colombia rages on and the United Nations reports that drug production is rising in the Andes. President Hugo Chávez increasingly polarizes Venezuela and the region, and uses oil hand-outs to prop up Fidel Castro's decrepit authoritarian regime in Cuba. Costa Rica's long-admired democratic system is torn by presidential scandals, Nicaragua may soon elect a failed Sandinista [leftist party member] from the past, and Haiti is a perpetual failure in every way.

Even Argentina, the market reform "model" in the 1990s, is on its sixth president in four years, five of them in a fortnight around New Year's Day, 2002. The economic collapse then devastated living standards for the majority and precipitated the largest debt default in world history, which was greeted with cheers in the national congress.

Why Democracy Fails

Polls show that democracy as a system is popular in the region, but also that most Latin Americans don't believe it works for them. Indeed, international agencies report that the region has long had the world's widest rich-poor gap and that living conditions and opportunities for bettering one's lot are few and in most places not increasing. And Latin America is falling ever farther behind the developing countries of Asia.

The problem of ineffective or downright failing democracies is far more basic to the region's thinking and governance

The Plagues of Latin American Democracies

Latin Americans have reason to be unhappy. The past few years have brought a spate of bad news. In 2002, economic activity contracted by about 1 percent regionwide, and in three countries plunged by 10 percent or more. Despite more than a decade of intense and often painful economic reforms, per-capita income has actually fallen since 1998 and, in most countries, is today [in 2003] about what it was in 1982. Unemployment is at record levels, now averaging some 50 percent higher in 2002 than it was a decade ago; in more than half a dozen countries—including Argentina, Colombia, Venezuela, and Uruguay—upwards of 15 percent of workers are without jobs. The region's halting social progress has stalled. Many economies remain trapped in up-and-down, roller-coaster cycles. Crime and violence are running rampant, and degrading the quality of life everywhere.

Compounding the impact of this dreary performance is the widespread view that national economies have been managed, not merely badly, but also unfairly. The perception—and all too often the reality—is that a tiny minority has been walking away with the gains while most people are getting poorer. With burgeoning numbers of high-priced cars, upscale malls, and luxury apartment complexes, much of Latin America looks far more prosperous than it did ten years ago. Yet as income statistics make clear, most citizens are no better off than they were one or two decades ago.

Peter Hakim, Journal of Democracy, *April 24, 2003.*

than politicians in the Americas—including Washington—are aware of or willing to admit.

Perhaps the main reason is because most Latin leaders and their cronies don't want to change a system that serves their private interests. And most policymakers in Washington concentrate so narrowly on a few yardsticks like periodic votes and trade agreements that they don't see (or acknowledge) what is really happening to people and why.

Instability, which seems so destructive of progress, is nothing new. Thirty years ago it was guerrilla wars, astronomical inflation, military governments, and human rights violations. Five hundred years ago it was conquest, virtual slavery, and mass exploitation under the guise of Catholic paternalism.

But that's not the point: Perpetual surface instability is not what causes Latin America's cycles of failure. The real problem is the opposite: excessive stability—the enduring legacy of Iberian [Spanish and Portuguese] colonialism ever modified to serve a new generation of leadership cliques.

Recalcitrant Leaders

For more than five centuries ruling cliques that took office—whether by colonial appointment, swords, bullets, or ballots—justified and maintained power with a culture and institutions that treated people as groups and denied most individuals the skills and opportunities to improve their lives. One of the very few things an overwhelming majority of people in all countries agreed on in a 2004 regional poll was that despite elections, power is held by cliques pursuing mainly their own interests.

The centuries of failure in Latin America stand in bleak contrast to the development successes in many Asian countries since World War II—and, more recently, even in Spain itself. In Asia, the basic changes in some cases were begun by authoritarian governments that in time became more democratic, as also happened in Chile from 1973 to 1990, when the current foundations of Latin America's most viable state were laid.

But very few democrats or others have ever made major permanent changes to benefit the people, and the failures of much-touted reforms in the 1990s laid the groundwork for increasing frustration and demagoguery today. The next few years are not likely to bring a rash of military coups, but mainly more democratic formalities that don't really serve the interests of the people.

One of Chile's main [Augusto] Pinochet-era reformers, José Piñera, has remarked that a country doesn't need authoritarianism to undertake basic reforms. And Peruvian analyst Alvaro Vargas Llosa argues the same in a recent book.

In short, Latin leaders must want substantive change and understand that the impediments to democracy and development in the past have not been bad individual leaders and their foreign allies but the region's own institutions and their culture.

Polls show decisively that Latin Americans want better housing, food, education, opportunities, and democracy. And there are now some democratic and market-oriented leaders who know well what needs to be done. As Mr. Vargas Llosa says, "Reform ultimately involves undoing more than doing." Government must be small, less intrusive, more efficient, more honest. Entrenched and corrupt entitlement programs must be eliminated. There must be greatly improved education for everyone, better healthcare and environmental standards, and legal reforms that guarantee opportunity, property, and other rights to all people.

It's up to reform-minded leaders to consolidate popular support for lasting and beneficial changes that will overcome the barriers to democracy and development imbedded in major aspects of Iberian culture and institutions.

| "Democracy in Latin America not only persists, but in many salient respects its quality has never been higher."

Democracy Persists in Latin America

Omar G. Encarnación

In the following viewpoint Omar G. Encarnación states that despite the economic and political crises that have plagued Latin America since the 1970s, democracy persists in the region. According to Encarnación, the staying power of democracy is attributable to the people's yearning for improved civil rights and political freedom. While he does not deny that the region is still mired in corruption and despotism, Encarnación contends that Latin America's governments have never been more participatory—a good sign for the continued evolution of democracy in these developing nations. Omar G. Encarnación is a professor of political studies at Bard College in New York.

As you read, consider the following questions:

1. According to the author, what percentage of Latin Americans polled by Latinobarómetro in 2002 agreed that democracy was preferable to other forms of government?

Omar G. Encarnación, "The Strange Persistence of Latin American Democracy," *World Policy Journal,* Winter 2003–2004, pp. 30–36. Copyright © 2003 by the World Policy Institute. Reproduced by permission.

2. What, in Encarnación's view, is "the most compelling indicator of democratic persistence in Latin America?"

In September 2001, while Americans were preoccupied with the aftermath of the terrorist attacks on New York and Washington, a remarkable economic and political story began to unfold in the southern cone of South America. That month, Argentina's economy, once praised by Wall Street, Washington, and international financial organizations as a model for the developing world, virtually imploded, sending the country into the worst economic crisis of its tumultuous history. The shocks to the economic system were severe: the collapse of an insolvent banking system, a default on international loans, a nearly 75 percent devaluation of the currency, and an economic contraction that drove the country's GDP [gross domestic product] back to 1993 levels. This economic meltdown proved devastating to what only a year previously had been Latin America's most prosperous nation. Most shocking was a poverty rate that swelled to 50 percent of the population, beggaring more than one and a half million people in just six months.

Equally dramatic was the toll the economic crisis took on the political system. Angered Argentines stormed banks and government offices in Buenos Aires and other urban centers, precipitating a rash of riots that claimed 21 lives. During this turmoil, no fewer than four different presidents sought to bring order to the nation between December 19, 2001, and January 2, 2002. Amid the chaos, there was a silver lining. The breakdown of democracy through a military coup—what we have come to expect in Argentina whenever civilian leaders are unable to cope with downturns in the economy and popular discontent—did not materialize. Indeed, the resilience of democracy was the most remarkable aspect of the economic crash in Argentina and a hopeful sign of "democratic consolidation" [in the words of Hector E. Schamis].

Democratic Resilience

Notwithstanding the disruptions prompted by multiple presidential resignations and hasty inaugurations, civilian leaders were able to keep the political system afloat. More importantly, people's faith in democracy did not falter. According to the polling data available from Latinobarómetro, a Santiago-based organization that has tracked political attitudes in Latin America since 1996, support for democracy in Argentina actually grew between 2001 and 2002. The percentage of Argentines that responded in the affirmative to the question "Is democracy preferable to any other kind of government?" increased from 58 percent in 2001 to 65 percent in 2002.

The survival of Argentine democracy is the most dramatic example of the remarkable persistence of constitutional rule in Latin America since the region began to shed its authoritarian regimes [in the 1970s], but it is not the only one. [In the early 1990s], besieged by hyperinflation, corruption, and widespread discontent with its political leaders, Brazil was at the top of the list of endangered democracies, and many observers predicted a democratic collapse triggered by a military coup. But the military has stayed in the barracks, and Brazil has seen one president succeed another in fair and open elections. This appears to be the case virtually everywhere in Latin America. At present, with the obvious exception of Communist Cuba, a democratically elected government presides in every country in the region. The surprising strength of democracy in Latin America has not gone unnoticed.

"The region has many problems," noted the *Economist* in a 2002 cover story, "but democracy, as such, is not among them." Astute commentators on the political scene echo this assessment. "The persistence of democracy in Latin America is remarkable and indeed a cause for celebration," writes Michael Shifter of Georgetown University's Center for Latin American Studies. Peter Hakim of the Inter-American Dialogue agrees: "The authoritarian option has become unthinkable in most of

Latin America today. The main concern is not whether democracy will survive in Latin America. It will. Rather what is at issue is the quality of governance and politics across Latin America."

Democracy's persistence in Latin America is easier to detect than to explain. Certainly, since the demise of communism in the early 1990s the climate for nondemocratic regimes has grown colder, while support for democracy has become the declared policy of the international development community and especially the U.S. government. Still, American support for democracy in Latin America in the last three decades has been oversold. This has notably been the case under George W. Bush, whose administration has made democratic promotion a key component of U.S. foreign policy. Moreover, most Latin American democracies operate in the absence of conditions usually deemed important for the sustainability of democracy: a healthy economy, credible and well-organized political institutions, and a thriving civil society. What accounts, then, for the persistence of democracy in Latin America?

Valuing Democratic Ideals

The answer seemingly derives, in large part, from a profound transformation of political attitudes. Latin Americans appear to value democratic governance for the political freedom and civil rights that accompany it above the social and economic benefits it may or may not deliver. This new political culture is indeed good news for Latin America since it shelters democracy from the failures and follies of elected leaders as well as from the vagaries of the economy. Yet, paradoxically, this newfound appreciation for democracy—born out of a process of political learning fueled by the fear of the return of authoritarian rule—may not necessarily bode well for the future because it can prevent governments from undertaking the

Democracy in Latin America

The [2004] report produced by the Program of the United Nations for Development . . . confirms that democracy is firmly in place. Democracy is understood as the way through which political personnel is chosen thanks to periodic, free, competitive, clean, electoral processes, under universal suffrage. This report places all the countries considered during the period of 1990–2002 inside the index of electoral democracy (defined by these variables: right to vote, integrity and freedom of elections, and elected public posts) within a bracket of .80 and 1. The only exceptions are Colombia (.57) and Guatemala (.60). The expansion of the democratic formula to the totality of Latin American countries, and for an estimable time period besides, is an historical moment given that this situation never took place before.

Manual Alcantara, Social Forces, June 2005.

very reforms needed to make democracy durable and effective.

The most compelling indicator of democratic persistence in Latin America is that not a single democratic transition [since the 1970s] has succumbed to an authoritarian reversal. This is no small achievement in a region where, historically, democracy's central dilemma has not been its absence (as in the Middle East) or its retarded development (as in Spain, Portugal, and Russia) but rather the inability of countries to make it stick. Since Latin America began experimenting with democratic governance in the mid-1800s, it has suffered from "pendulum syndrome," that is, from periodic and often violent swings between democratic governance and authoritarian rule. This accounts for Latin America's deserved reputation for political instability.

Democracy in Latin America not only persists, but in many salient respects its quality has never been higher. According to Freedom House, whose surveys of political and civil rights have become acknowledged standards for calibrating the quality of democracy worldwide, "the scale of political progress in Latin America in the last three decades has been dramatic." The organization's most recent report notes that in 1972, when it conducted its first survey, the Americas and the Caribbean had 13 "free" (read fully democratic), 9 "partly free," and 4 "not free" countries. By contrast, today this region has 23 "free," 10 "partly free," and 2 (Cuba and Haiti) "not free" countries.

The Freedom House data mirror the extent to which democratic institutions and practices have been broadly accepted in Latin America. With few exceptions, fair elections, the hallmark of the democratic process, were a rarity in the region prior to the 1980s. Corruption was so widespread that disputes over electoral results were a major source of chronic ferment. [In the new millennium], genuinely competitive elections are the order of the day. Tina Rosenberg of the *New York Times,* writing from Mexico, where elections have traditionally been "the stuff of global infamy," reports that Mexico's electoral institute now advises other countries on how to conduct clean balloting. "On the basics, like registration, voting and counting ballots," she writes, "Mexico probably does better than the United States." A representative of the U.S. Federal Election Commission who traveled to Brazil to observe that country's 2002 presidential election declared the Brazilian electoral system "outstanding" and a model of technological prowess, transparency, and efficiency—no small feat considering that Brazil's electorate exceeds 110 million people.

More Participation

Another key indicator is that Latin American political life has never been more inclusive and participatory. The wave of democratization that began in the late 1970s can rightly be credited with mobilizing and enfranchising previously underrepresented social classes, minorities, and ethnic groups. In Brazil, an ostensibly democratic regime that was ousted by a military coup in 1964 denied the franchise to illiterates (a vast portion of the population) and banned the Communist Party, egregious violations redressed by a subsequent democratic regime that came to power in 1985. In several Andean countries, indigenous peoples acquired full political rights for the first time with the enactment of new democratic constitutions in the 1980s and 1990s.

The new democratic era has also witnessed the decentralization of political authority. In 1989, Venezuelans voted for governors for the first time in their country's history. In 1994, residents of Buenos Aires went to the polls for the first time to elect a mayor; Mexico City residents voted for mayor for the first time in 1997. In Brazilian cities governed by the Workers' Party, such as Porto Allegre and Betim, citizen participation in local government has increased dramatically with the introduction of "participatory democracy" programs that allow ordinary people a voice in local government, including setting budgetary priorities. . . .

To be sure, "democratic persistence" is not to be confused with "democratic consolidation," that seemingly elusive status that makes democratic institutions immune to decay and collapse. Consider recent events in the Andean region (Venezuela, Ecuador, Colombia, Peru, and Bolivia) where reckless populism, guerrilla activity, left-wing insurrections, and military coups serve as a powerful reminder that Latin America's familiar political demons have hardly been exorcised. . .

Latin America's newly found attachment to democracy, however imperfect and unlovely it may be, is rooted in a process of political learning emanating from prior democratic failure. The political elites that reconstructed democratic politics in Latin America appear determined to avoid the ideological polarization of the past (whether provoked by the right or the left), which often reduced politics to a zero-sum game.

| "*Democracy is, more and more, asserting its presence in the region.*"

Democracy Is Spreading in Asia

Anwar Ibrahim

Anwar Ibrahim served as the deputy prime minister of Malaysia from 1993 to 1998. After being dismissed in 1998, he was tried for corruption and jailed for six years. He regained his freedom in 2004. Despite his belief that his case was a miscarriage of justice, Ibrahim argues in the following viewpoint that the reign of Asian leaders who would subvert democracy and tamper with justice is drawing to a close. As some Asian countries embrace democracy, they inspire neighboring nations to press for social reforms. Ibrahim predicts that eventually the tide will be too strong for autocratic regimes to stay in power.

As you read, consider the following questions:

1. What does Ibrahim credit with ending the dictator Suharto's rule in Indonesia?

2. According to the author, what practice of ASEAN national leaders is keeping the organization from instituting regional standards for democracy?

3. What does Ibrahim say "nourishes the desire for things higher than mere physical comfort?"

Anwar Ibrahim, "The Quest for Social Justice," *Global Agenda,* vol. 3, January 2005.

Hope for Justice and Democracy

How many have suffered when justice is miscarried? Celebrated victims ... may be remembered and given their place in history, but what happens to the rest? Must they remain faceless and simply disappear?

According to legend, Pandora's box, which released plague, disease, sorrow and all manner of evil to the world, also contains the counterbalance called Hope. When pain inflicts, hope consoles.

Hope may be the most irrational of human instincts, but it is what makes us human. To the many who are unjustly incarcerated, it is hope that preserves their humanity. Some hope for justice beyond the grave, and some hope the world will become a better place so that others will not suffer as they have.

I too have such hopes, which I carried with me out of prison, along with my toothbrush and bundle of clothes.

When the Supreme Court [of Malaysia] announced my freedom, I felt a shot of euphoria surging through my veins. But it was a temporary high. As it began to wear off, I realized that although I was free from the cold stares of four grey walls, there were other walls, more insidious, surrounding me and my compatriots. I may be free to socialize with family and friends, but in my mind's ear, I hear the rattle of chains that seek to shackle our thoughts and imagination.

If you were walking out of prison after serving a lengthy term, you would more than likely experience the curious, eerie feeling of stepping into a different time zone, as if you had an internal clock that ran at a slower pace than real time.

As a prisoner, I felt as if the world rolled to a dull, lethargic rhythm. It was a world in which death was more real and more certain, for among its inhabitants were convicted murderers and drug traffickers (Malaysian law makes the death sentence mandatory for those caught in possession of narcot-

The U.S. Commitment to East Asia and the Pacific

The United States is committed to encouraging governments to develop pluralistic and representative democracies, supporting the formation of transparent and accountable legal systems, and to strengthening civil society organizations capable of holding the Government accountable. The development of free societies characterized by respect for international human rights standards, democratic institutions, a mature civil society, religious freedom and the rule of law is a critical U.S. foreign policy objective in East Asia and the Pacific. The United States encourages respect for worker rights in accordance with international labor standards, ensuring that economic growth will not be at the expense of the welfare of workers. The United States has stressed to countries throughout Asia the necessity of fighting the war on terrorism in a manner consistent with respect for human rights.

U.S. Department of State, Bureau of Democracy, Human Rights, and Labor, Supporting Human Rights and Democracy: The U.S. Record 2004–2005, *March 28, 2005.*

ics above a specified amount).

But it was also a world of wayward boys accused of some misdemeanour or other, languishing as they await trial. The wait would often last two years or more—longer than the prison terms they would have served had they pleaded guilty.

Prisons are built to isolate criminals from the rest of us. And society often forgets its prisoners and their existential situation. Among the forgotten are innocents who, because of a lapse or corruption in the system, are thrown in to share the life of the condemned.

Lapses in the administration of justice can happen anywhere, even in societies claiming the best system humanly possible. But in some societies the miscarriage of justice has become endemic and is sometimes used as a convenient political tool. My court trials and six-year incarceration, for example, had all the facade of legality and procedural justice, but only for the naive. In essence, the whole saga was just a more sophisticated version of the Moscow show trial.

Aside from political persecution masked by legal procedure, we also have variations of gulags (Soviet forced labour camps) and political prisons, especially in Asia and Africa. It is amazing how stubbornly these camps of shame survive. They certainly serve well the sinister political purposes of those in power.

In the world outside prison, time is an Olympian sprinter. The Asian currency crisis and economic meltdown [in the 1990s]—the backdrop to my incarceration—are now a distant memory. Thailand and South Korea, among the worst hit by the crisis, are again economic powerhouses. For Indonesia, the crisis was cataclysmic, but it terminated Suharto's military rule, forced open the gate to genuine democracy, and unleashed a free press and a vibrant civil society.

As I write this, I am preparing for a trip to Jakarta. I have much to learn from old friends there. I want to hear them tell me what it is like to ride the wind of change. Indonesia, which for three decades was ruled by a military autocracy, is now the Muslim world's biggest democracy. What a great thing this is at a time when Muslims are often branded as inherently antidemocratic. There is still a lot to be done, of course. Indonesia has to provide a decent living to some 220 million souls while combating destructive elements such as ethnic or religious bigots. Indonesian Muslims are known for their moderation and have embraced modernity with eagerness, but acts of terrorism have marred that image.

Dividends from Crisis

The economic crisis of the late 1990s was not without its dividends. It was the shock treatment that east Asians needed to make them see the need for reform. The countries that learnt their lessons and reformed their economies are now poised for greater heights. Before the crisis, the resistance was strong against calls for transparency in governance and business. That has changed somewhat. There is some consensus, at least in words if not yet in deeds, that opacity is bad for business, be it the business of governing or the business of making money.

This is not to say that forces resistant to reform and un-friendly to democracy have simply surrendered. On the contrary, they have tried to strengthen their positions. The [2005] decision by the Myanmar junta [military government] to extend the house arrest on [pro-democracy advocate] Daw Aung San Suu Kyi is a case in point. Other countries pay lip service to democracy while their policies ensure that the playing field becomes increasingly uneven. The press remains submissive to the ruling clique and fundamental liberties are severely curtailed.

One of the dividends of the crisis is that the struggle for freedom has taken on a regional character. The civil society sector is forging regional solidarity for democracy and human rights. The governments of [the] Association of Southeast Asian Nations (ASEAN)—the 10-nation regional grouping—are fearful of this new development and cling stubbornly to their outmoded doctrine of non-intervention in the domestic affairs of member-states.

Democracy Is Contagious

ASEAN is replete with internal contradictions. Some of its members—Indonesia, the Philippines, Thailand—have made giant leaps into mature democracy. But they have not made a serious effort to influence their less democratic partners, or to put democracy on the ASEAN agenda. The ASEAN leaders are proud of their tradition of consensual decision-making, but this is the very thing that keeps the group inert, that makes it unwilling to set a standard of democratic governance that it could impose on member-states.

But freedom has a demonstrative effect. ASEAN leaders must wake up to the reality that democracy is, more and more, asserting its presence in the region. The democratic mind is nurtured by social and political activism and by unlimited access to information. We are seeing the birth of an informed ASEANese community. It will be increasingly evident to ASEAN citizens that authoritarianism limits their choices and only democracy is capable of meeting their demand for greater choice.

The desire for freedom is universal, and the appetite for it is whetted when one sees others enjoying their liberties. Malaysians are more economically successful than Indonesians, but they envy their southern cousins for their political freedoms. They dream of the day when their television, radio and newspapers are as free as those found in Indonesia, Thailand and the Philippines. This Malaysian dream is shared by other ASEANese living under tight autocratic regimes.

It was the Cold War that brought the original five ASEAN countries together as a purely political grouping subscribing to "peace, freedom and neutrality". With the end of the Cold War, it was inevitable that economics would take precedence over politics. And as the economies of the region become more interlinked, so do the fates of the ASEAN peoples.

ASEAN is diverse, but there are fundamental cultural, economic and political meeting points. The desire for wealth is a common motivation, and it has resulted in high economic growth in the region, albeit uneven. But economic well-being has an effect unintended by some of the ASEAN policy- makers. It nourishes the desire for things higher than mere physical comfort. Such higher needs are associated with freedom.

Current ASEAN leaders want to set limits to their cooperation. They should know that they are daydreaming. Deepening economic integration will bring with it many unintended consequences. It is not only the ASEANese desire for democracy, openness and freedom that they will have to grapple with. It may not be too long before the peoples of the region begin to see themselves as members of a single community. When that happens, the seed of ASEAN greatness will have been sown.

> *"Elected regimes in East Asia are failing to deliver equity to their citizens."*

Democracy Is Being Undermined in Asia

Hilton L. Root

In the following viewpoint Hilton L. Root argues that the economic crisis in East Asia during the late 1990s prompted many nondemocratic, business-oriented regimes to provide for greater social and political freedoms. However, in the aftermath of the crisis, in Root's view, democratically elected leaders are not living up to expectations. According to Root, the moneyed elite are now buying out the leaders and revoking many of the progressive reforms that the new governments had passed in the bleak years of crisis. The result has been a challenge to the fledgling democracies in developing nations. Hilton L. Root is a former professor who has served as an advisor to the World Bank, the International Monetary Fund, and the U.S. Treasury.

As you read, consider the following questions:

1. As Root notes, how did South Korean leader Kim Dae Jung succumb to business elites?

2. In the author's view, why do observers fear that Indonesian president Megawati Sukarnoputri will be re-

stricted in her ability to defend human rights in her nation?

3. What is the "authoritarian hangover," as Root describes it?

B etween 1960 and 1997, East Asia's high-performing economies consistently grew faster than the world rate of growth. This remarkable record rests in part on innovations in policy and governance made by governments in Indonesia, Malaysia, the Philippines, Singapore, South Korea, Taiwan, and Thailand. Now, in the wake of the late 1990s financial crisis and in the midst of a worldwide economic downturn, these governments must make tough policy choices, some of which may upset the very groups who were the biggest "winners" from the high-growth years. What insights should guide today's leaders as they work to restore a unified commitment to genuine national development? How can democratic principles assist them in this task?

Anxious to counter Chinese belligerence and the spread of communism during the Cold War, East Asian leaders realized the need to craft strategic social compromises within their own societies. They adopted innovations in governance in order to reduce social divisions. While the primary intention may have been political, there were huge material benefits as well, for these reforms laid the groundwork for the extraordinary economic success that the region would enjoy throughout almost the whole of the late twentieth century.

Fearing enemies at the gate, elites throughout East Asia made short-term sacrifices in authority, rents, and privileges in order to improve the living standards of the rural poor and the working class. Convinced that economic failure could lead to national disintegration, the leaders of these countries gave technocrats authority over economic policy. With national survival demanding collaboration among different social strata, narrow redistributive goals gave way to more inclusive policies that required sacrifice and coordination to produce broad-based benefits. The resulting social cohesion—unique in the developing world—helped motivate East Asian populations to learn, to innovate, and to absorb new ideas.

Growth favoring one group over another would have undermined the political bargain needed to sustain national economic policies. Therefore government-sponsored credit schemes for business and industry were accompanied by improved access to jobs, housing, health care, and education for ordinary workers and citizens. This two-pronged approach was wise and *necessary*, but in recent years its once-hidden downside has become plain. Many firms favored for decades with political access and subsidized credit have become hothouse flowers, feeble and uncompetitive. Continuing to prop them up has involved unappetizing choices and high social costs, but standing by while established and prestigious firms flounder or even go under has also not been easy for officials to do. Policy makers throughout the region have continued to wrestle with this dilemma.

Conflict and Discontent

Ominously, in the years since the financial crisis of 1997, we have seen the East Asian capitals of Manila, Seoul, Bangkok, Kuala Lumpur, and Jakarta rocked by violent, class-tinged street demonstrations. Likewise, the Philippines, South Korea, Thailand, Malaysia, and Indonesia have all experienced a resurgence of regionalism in politics. The sprawling island nations of Indonesia and the Philippines are both facing strong secessionist movements.

Why are these things happening, and why now? One explanation is that at the end of the Cold War, East Asian leaders shifted gears, quietly downgrading the need to maintain the implicit social bargain. The result has been internal discontent and a consequent frustration of the very policy reforms needed to restore growth. These domestic schisms, even more than external threats, are the gravest threat to regional stability. Has increasing democracy, as some critics maintain, helped to bring these schisms to a head? Are there ways in which democracy can actually bolster social cohesion?

Ineffective Leadership

Many say that the region's democratically elected leaders do not measure up to their authoritarian predecessors, who often oversaw the periods of fastest growth. Today's leaders, these critics claim, lack the will to implement bold and badly needed policy initiatives in their crisis-stricken states. These charges are far from baseless. The elected officials who came to power in Indonesia, South Korea, Taiwan, and Thailand after the financial crisis of 1997 all had strong reformist credentials and were thought to be highly qualified to improve governance and restore a unified commitment to genuine national development. Yet three years later, these same leaders have squandered opportunities to bring about change and have not delivered the reforms they promised.

Even the most successful . . . East Asian leader, Nobel Peace laureate Kim Dae Jung of South Korea [who left office in 2003], failed in his promise to rein in Daewoo, Hyundai, Samsung, and other powerful *chaebols* (conglomerates). Instead, President Kim allowed a handful of tycoons to block public scrutiny of their companies' accounts. He forged an unlikely alliance with his long-time enemy Kim Jong Pil, an archconservative who was prime minister during the dictatorship of President Park Chung Hee (1961–79). Such compromises with the enemies of change, common throughout the region, mortgage the future by deferring badly needed reforms in the name of immediate political survival.

Setbacks in Thailand and Elsewhere

After coming to power in 1997 with an overwhelming mandate, Thai prime minister Chuan Leekpai's Democrats fell vic-

Latecomers to Democracy

India, Pakistan, and Sri Lanka gained independence at the beginning of [the second] wave [of worldwide democratization, 1945–1964], and Malaysian independence in 1957 might be regarded as part of it, but democratization in most of East and Southeast Asia was confined to the third wave in the late 1980s and 1990s. It is probably too early to judge the significance of this for the effectiveness of democratic consolidation, but non-participation in the second wave, when South Korea, Taiwan, the Philippines, and Indonesia were still under authoritarian rule, means that experience of democracy is more limited than in much of Africa. There has not been the same process of trial and error that may enable democrats to spot authoritarian threats, especially from the army or the ruling party, or to strengthen democratic safeguards, such as freedom of the press and the careful monitoring of elections.

Robert Pinkney, Democracy in the Third World, *2003.*

tim to many of the same special-interest pressures that had corrupted previous governments. In January 2001, the opposition Thai Rak Thai ("Thais Love Thais") party, backed by moneyed interests, turned the Democrats out in elections and promised to wipe out many of the recent reforms. The new prime minister, Thaksin Shinawatra, openly embraces business oligarchs who trade on the basis of personal reputation and social networks, and place little value on strengthening the creaky set of legal procedures and institutions that Thailand uses to handle bankruptcy cases. As many as a hundred of his party's candidates allegedly cheated in races where millions of dollars went to buy villagers' votes. As if to add insult to the Democrats' injury, the victorious Thaksin announced that he would form a coalition with two traditional rural-based parties run by ex-premiers whose tenures were noted for disastrously poor governance: the New Aspiration Party of Chaovalit Yongchaiyut and the Chart Thai party of Banharn Silpa-Archa.

Elsewhere in the region, disturbingly similar stories unfolded. In Malaysia, Prime Minister Mahathir bin Mohamad has been accused of reverting to crony privatization by bailing out the same politically connected firms whose poor management triggered the country's crisis in 1997. In the Philippines, impeached president Joseph Estrada disappointed the poor who elected him by compromising economic reform for personal gain. He promised to protect the downtrodden, but robbed them instead. The irregular manner in which he was driven from office and his replacement by establishment figure Gloria Macapagal Arroyo brought the poor into the streets to protest giving old vested interests privileged access to the presidential palace. As frustration mounts, violent revolutionary movements grow. The New People's Army more than doubled in size between 1995 and 2001. and is now said to have more than 11,000 troops. The Islamic Abu Sayyaf movement is also gaining strength. Reform was also difficult in Taiwan. Chen Shui-bian, the former mayor of Taipei who was elected president in March 2000, faced impeachment charges from old-line politicians who rejected even modest proposals for change. To increase his prospects for reelection, he too may have to forgo many of his reformist ambitions.

Troubles in Indonesia

The most embattled leader of all was Indonesia's Abdurrahman Wahid, a visionary with a long record of standing up for human rights during the 31 years of Suharto's dictatorship. His powerful rivals, including many holdovers from Suharto's New Order regime, resorted to terror campaigns in their struggle to regain power and prevent the prosecution of Suharto-era crimes. Nevertheless, by the time he was driven from office in mid-2001, Wahid had compromised his integrity in the eyes of many of his supporters by holding back-room talks with the same wealthy Chinese conglomerate own-ers whom he publicly castigated for their Suharto connections. As a result, these conglomerates' bankrupted assets were nei-ther restructured nor sold while under government control. Many fear that they will wind up back in the hands of their original owners as a result of sweetheart deals backed by gov-ernment loans.

Wahid's successor, Megawati Sukarnoputri, gained stature by keeping her independence from Suharto. Yet to supplant Wahid she built close ties to the former dictator's loyalists, in-cluding his political party, Golkar, and the armed forces. Many fear that her dependence on Indonesia's powerful and politi-cally active military will restrict her ability to defend human rights and will mean that the generals behind the suppression of East Timor will never be brought to justice.

Similarly, many fear that Megawati's ascension to the presi-dency will stall the battle against corruption because she can-not afford to challenge members of her own coalition. Megawati's willingness to make peace with the forces that kept Suharto in power comes at a price: Strengthening the legal and judicial system is a cause likely to find few supporters among her core backers. How can she be expected to devote her attention to resolving the country's most serious difficul-ties with bad debts while trying to hold on to the approval of political elites who grew rich from Suharto-era corruption? [Sukarnoputri failed to win reelection in 2004.] . . .

Why do Indonesia's elected leaders keep courting the very elites that have led the country into bankruptcy and social conflict and that continue to deny the need for reform? Wahid's and Megawati's courting of moneyed interests is in-dicative of leadership trends throughout East Asia. Wahid, many believe, was simply trying to raise enough money for the 2004 presidential campaign. But in trying to create a sus-tainable political base, he ended up failing to resolve any of the nation's pressing problems. In this regard, Wahid's failure, his inability to surmount the entrenched interests of the past to make the right choices for the future, may be the rule rather than the exception in East Asia. . . .

The Legacy of Powerful Business

Adding to the region's woes is the erosion of states' power to foster the collaboration needed to support economic policies that benefit the whole of society. Even with Western lectures on the evils of state-led development ringing in their ears, many East Asians have mixed feelings about having central bureaucracies hand over power to the corporate sector. Many East Asian countries lack the smooth-functioning legal systems usually associated with high-growth economies and they have relied on able bureaucrats to fill the gap. Now we are seeing bureaucracies lose power while legal systems remain weak and good governance suffers. Public authorities will find it hard to enforce contracts, and investment flows will diminish. In Suharto-era Indonesia, for instance, investors knew that the strongman and his Chinese cronies—if properly cultivated—would safeguard investments and enforce contracts. That personalized mechanism vanished from the scene along with Suharto, and no one really believes that Indonesia's attenuated legal system can adequately uphold the integrity of contracts. . . .

The hard truth is that authoritarianism, whatever its sins, did foster well-developed organs of public administration. One need not wish for authoritarianism's return in order to point out that democratic governments must find lawful, peaceful ways to stop wealthy minorities from distorting public policy to serve their own ends. Civil society, regrettably, still suffers from an authoritarian hangover (social mobilization always required government approval), and so in this crucial struggle its effectiveness is limited. Interest intermediation is restricted to a few narrow, elite-dominated channels.

Civil society groups tend to be too thin on the ground, too poorly organized, and too weakly represented to ensure that public institutions are used to uphold public interests rather than to maintain the power of ruling coalitions.

The absence of a strong civil society to counterbalance the power of the wealthy is also a big reason why democratically elected regimes in East Asia are failing to deliver equity to their citizens or to implement effective reform programs. The concentration of economic power in firms with a history of political connections creates conditions that lend themselves to corruption. Corporate owners and officials, anxious for continued special treatment, can and do tempt judges, politicians, civil servants, and other agents of the state with huge bribes. The wealth that these corporate interests dispose of is itself the result of previous government interventions in their favor. The current holders of this wealth know that paying for more such interventions is the key to continued fortune. In this environment, governments are challenged to build institutions that can oversee and regulate economic activity with an eye to promoting fairness, accountability, healthy competition, and the public weal. The result is popular frustration, resentment, and, ultimately, political instability.

Periodical Bibliography

The following articles have been selected to supplement the diverse views presented in this chapter.

Yu-Ping Chan — "Democracy or Bust? The Development Dilemma," *Harvard International Review*, Fall 2001.

Economist — "Liberty's Great Advance," June 28, 2003.

Amy L. Freedman — "Economic Crises and Political Change: Indonesia, South Korea, and Malaysia," *World Affairs*, Spring 2004.

Terry Gibbs — "Democracy's Crisis of Legitimacy in Latin America," *NACLA Report on the Americas*, July/August 2004.

Jeff Haynes — "Democratic Consolidation in the Third World: Many Questions, Any Answers?" *Contemporary Politics*, June 2000.

Amartya Sen — "Democracy and Its Global Roots," *New Republic*, October 6, 2003.

Doh Chull Shin and Jason Wells — "Is Democracy the Only Game in Town," *Journal of Democracy*, April 2005.

Joseph T. Siegle, Michael M. Weinstein, and Morton H. Halperin — "Why Democracies Excel," *Foreign Affairs*, September/October 2004.

Christopher Skene — "Authoritarian Practices in New Democracies," *Journal of Contemporary Asia*, 2003.

Mark R. Thompson — "Pacific Asia After 'Asian Values': Authoritarianism, Democracy, and 'Good Governance,'" *Third World Quarterly*, vol. 25, no. 6, 2004.

Jennifer Widner — "Africa's Democratization: A Work in Progress," *Current History*, May 2005.

CHAPTER 4

How Should the United States Assist the Third World?

Chapter Preface

In March 2002, the presidential administration of George W. Bush developed the Millennium Challenge Account (MCA), a new method of disbursing U.S. aid to developing nations. Under the MCA, the administration would choose which nations to award large aid commitments (for economic development only) based on the quality of "good governance" demonstrated by the recipients. This plan was instituted in reaction to a steadfast belief that most U.S. aid was never reaching needy populations and was instead simply lining the pockets of corrupt dictators and government officials in the Third World. In 2004, the Bush administration picked its first sixteen countries that met the good governance requirements. They were the nations of Armenia, Benin, Bolivia, Cape Verde, Georgia, Ghana, Honduras, Lesotho, Madagascar, Mali, Mongolia, Mozambique, Nicaragua, Senegal, Sri Lanka, and Vanuatu.

Besides insisting on good governance, the MCA requires these aid recipients to lower or disband tariffs and business protections and open markets to global trade. As President Bush asserted in 2004 regarding the MCA's predicted impact on developing nations, "The powerful combination of trade and open markets and good government is history's proven method to defeat poverty on a large scale, to vastly improve health and education, to build a modern infrastructure while safeguarding the environment, and to spread the habits of liberty and enterprise." But as the president warned, "Funding is not guaranteed for any selected country. To be awarded a grant, nations must develop proposals explaining how they will further address the needs of their people and increase economic growth, proposals that set clear goals and measurable benchmarks." If a selected nation fails to honor its pledges, U.S. aid is still available to them through older institutions such as the U.S. Agency for International Development (USAID) that utilize governmental and nongovernmental funds. Even developing states not chosen for MCA funds can still receive aid through these channels. However, the administration hopes that the benefits of globalization and government aid packages will induce other nations that may lack good governance to reform their politics and aspire to MCA rewards.

This new U.S. assistance policy has its champions and its critics. In the following chapter, commentators debate the effectiveness of the Millennium Challenge Account as well as other ways in which the United States is helping or hindering development of the Third World.

| "Levels of assistance ... must be more clearly linked to a country's developmental performance and to the quality of its governance."

U.S. Aid Should Target Nations That Practice Good Governance

Andrew Natsios and Larry Diamond

In the following viewpoint Andrew Natsios and Larry Diamond argue that outmoded U.S. aid programs funnel money to corrupt governments that do nothing to better the plight of their people. In response, Natsios and Diamond support the Millennium Challenge Account (MCA)—a program developed by the George W. Bush administration that distributes aid based on the good governance of recipient nations. The authors attest that this type of aid program will ensure that no more money is wasted on despotic leaders and faulty governments and instead will force recipients to adhere to criteria that will benefit the development of their nations. Andrew Natsios is the administrator of the United States Agency for International Development. Larry Diamond is a senior fellow at the Hoover Institution, a conservative think tank.

As you read, consider the following questions:

1. According to the authors, what three broad criteria are used by the MCA to determine if a developing nation deserves aid?

2. If a developing nation's government ignores the "good governance" criteria of the MCA, how will the United States still get some aid to the people of that nation, according to Natsios and Diamond?

3. Besides ensuring good governance, what other facets of development do Natsios and Diamond say the United States will tackle in its disbursement of aid?

Since [Iraqi dictator] Saddam Hussein's fall from power [in] April [2003], the world has learned a great deal about the consequences of his abhorrent rule: mass killings, a brutalized population, staggering corruption, an impoverished population, a devastated environment, neglected educational institutions, a miscarried justice system, and other failing governmental functions. This legacy of Saddam's horrific misrule is the most dramatic demonstration of the vital connection between the vibrancy and economic development of a people and the nature of their governing institutions. The mounting evidence of this linkage around the world must drive a revolution in the way that we administer foreign assistance.

Saddam Hussein's Iraq was merely the most recent example of atrocious governance in a world filled with dozens of tyrannical, predatory, and failing states. Democratic and accountable states do significantly better at delivering development for their people. To be sure, some East Asian states have contained corruption and achieved rapid development under authoritarian rule—but worldwide, these states have been the exception. Over the past two decades, the two most rapidly developing countries in Africa have been the only two African states to sustain democracy continuously since independence, Botswana and Mauritius. Recent research by Richard Roll and

John Talbott (published in the July 2003 *Journal of Democracy*) shows that government institutions and policies explain most of the variation across countries in economic development, with property rights, control of corruption, civil liberties, and political rights all significant factors accounting for development success. Thomas Zweifel and Patricio Navarro find (in the same issue of the *Journal of Democracy*) that at every level of national development, fewer infants die in democracies than in dictatorships.

Corruption Stalls Development

In too many countries around the world, government does not advance the common good. Decisions benefit the rulers, their clans, oligarchies, and party but not the people. Corruption is rampant, laws are trampled, state capacity is weak, infrastructure is poor, and social services are starved. Jobs are scarce because investment is scant in the face of predatory governments and insecure property rights. Consequently, development is stalled and people are impoverished, alienated, and angry.

Our national interest urgently requires that we confront these scandalous betrayals of development promise. But decades of experience have taught us that we cannot do so by simply throwing money at the problem. No amount of resources transferred or infrastructure built can compensate for—or survive—rotten governance. Lifting countries out of poverty and hopelessness requires fundamental reforms to make governments more transparent, inclusive, lawful, and responsible to their citizens. These reforms can be sustained, deepened, and even catalyzed by clear rewards for governments that demonstrate a genuine commitment to human development and good governance. But linking aid emphatically to governments' development performance and policy commitment is a radical step. Indeed, it entails a revolution in foreign assistance.

Criteria for MCA Eligibility

The [Millennium Challenge Account] Board will make use of sixteen indicators to assess policy performance of individual countries. These indicators are grouped . . . under the three policy categories as follows:

Ruling Justly:	Encouraging Economic Freedom:	Investing in People:
1. Civil Liberties	1. Country Credit Rating	1. Public Expenditures on Health as Percent of GDP
2. Political Rights	2. 1-year Consumer Price Inflation	2. Immunization Rates: DPT3 and Measles
3. Voice and Accountability	3. Fiscal Policy	3. Public Primary Education Spending as Percent of GDP
4. Government Effectiveness	4. Trade Policy	4. Primary Education Completion Rate
5. Rule of Law	5. Regulatory Quality	
6. Control of Corruption	6. Days to Start a Business	

In making its determination of eligibility with respect to a particular candidate country, the Board will consider whether such country performs above the median in relation to its peers on at least half of the indicators in each of the three policy categories and above the median on the corruption indicator. One exception to these relative comparisons is inflation, for which a country needs to pass an absolute test of having an inflation rate under 20%.

Millennium Challenge Corporation, "Report on the Criteria and Methodology for Determining the Eligibility of Candidate Countries for Millennium Challenge Account Assistance in FY 2004." www.mcc.gov/countries/selection/methodology_report.pdf.

The Tough Love Approach

The Bush administration has already taken a bold step in that revolution with the creation of the Millennium Challenge Account, which will allocate $5 billion a year in new development assistance to the less developed countries that perform best on three broad criteria: ruling justly, investing in people, and encouraging economic freedom. But the drive for more just and responsible governance must infuse all our development assistance efforts—and not just those of the United States but of other bilateral and multilateral donors as well.

The old approach of conditionality—providing aid and then hoping that governments will comply with its expectations—has run its course. We must move from conditionality to selectivity, and from a motivation of unconditional obligation to a "tough love" approach that manifests a more profound compassion because it demands results. The president's Millennium Challenge Account is the first step toward this new development construct, and these principles must now be embodied throughout U.S. development assistance programs.

The following elements are crucial to success. Levels of assistance, particularly development assistance as opposed to humanitarian relief or emergency health programs, must be more clearly linked to a country's development performance and to the quality of its governance in controlling corruption and ensuring freedom and democracy. Good performers need to be tangibly rewarded with increased development assistance from the international community, more far-reaching debt relief, incentives for foreign investment, and trade liberalization. Democratic, accountable governance with responsible economic policies should bring immediate, significant, and sustained benefits.

If corrupt, abusive governments show no political commitment to democratic reforms and good governance, the United States will work primarily with nongovernmental actors instead. At the same time, where we can identify committed reformers within a corrupt state, we should work with them, provide them assistance, and try to strengthen their hand.

It is vital that the other development assistance donors embrace this logic of expecting and rewarding open and accountable governance. The United States must lead the global development community to preclude providing development assistance to grossly corrupt and abusive governments while enhancing aid to governments that sustain political and economic reform. The bilateral donors should mount coordinated efforts to pressure bad governments and to cut off the flows of assistance that keep venal, oppressive governments afloat. These governments—and their people—must hear a firm and consistent message from the international community. The game of promising reform and then stealing public resources, locking up the press, rigging elections, and subverting the rule of law is over. The time for reform is now.

Ensuring Success

If this new, governance-led approach to assistance is going to work, it must provide effective democracy and governance assistance programs. These programs must mobilize strong links among donors, across government agencies, across sectors, and across different developing countries to tackle a number of key challenges:

- Strengthening the institutions of public accountability that monitor and control corruption

- Institutionalizing the rule of law through judicial reform, human rights work, and more professional and democratic policing

- Strengthening and democratizing political parties and deepening their roots in society

- Assisting democratic groups and media in civil society to become more effective advocates of reform and to develop broader societal constituencies

- Developing stronger, more professional states that can

respond to rising demands for more responsible governance

More accountable and democratic governance will not in itself deliver development. The revolution in foreign aid has many other dimensions as well, such as renewing the commitment to education and improved agricultural productivity, assisting countries to streamline their regulations and lower trade barriers, and supporting the microeconomic reforms that build a competitive business environment and an entrepreneurial class. It involves changes in health assistance to respond to the increase in noncommunicable diseases and the HIV/AIDS epidemic. And it entails integrated and context-sensitive policies to respond to civil conflicts and humanitarian emergencies in failed and failing states.

The United States has a moral and political responsibility to respond rapidly in the face of famine and humanitarian disaster. But as [Nobel Prize–winning economist] Amartya Sen has shown [in his book *Poverty and Famines*], famines do not take place in democracies. And countries that are well and decently governed do not fall victim to civil war. The best policy for managing violent conflict is to prevent it, through the construction of inclusive, just, democratic, and accountable governments. All the other lessons and imperatives of development assistance depend on this fundamental condition of governance for their sustainable success. And it is this realization that lies at the core of the revolution in development thinking and policy.

> *"The emphasis on good governance means that the benefits of the [aid] program will go to countries that already enjoy a high level of state capacity."*

U.S. Aid Should Not Target Nations That Practice Good Governance

Neil A. Englehart

Neil A. Englehart is a professor of government and law at Lafayette College in Pennsylvania. In the following viewpoint he discusses what he perceives as the shortcomings of the Millennium Challenge Account (MCA), the new foreign aid program that targets aid to nations showing promise in good governance. Englehart opposes favoring well-governed nations because they are the ones most likely to succeed without foreign support. The developing countries troubled by human rights abuses and corruption need the most help, he insists, but under the MCA they are the ones most likely to be ignored.

As you read, consider the following questions:

1. Why does Englehart believe that the Millennium Challenge Corporation will likely not be any more efficient than other U.S. aid programs?

Neil A. Engelhart, "Picking Winners: The Millennium Challenge Accounts," *Dissent*, Fall 2004 pp. 74–77. Copyright © 2004 by the Dissent Publishing Corporation. Reproduced by permission.

2. What is the Human Development Index, according to the author, and how do most of the worst-governed states rank on this index?

3. What addendum to the MCA does Englehart propose, and why does he believe it is needed?

Having identified weak and failing states as a significant threat to both U.S. security interests and the international order, the Bush administration has failed to formulate any strategy for dealing with these states. Its new foreign aid initiative replicates this failure, targeting aid to the best-governed low-income states while ignoring the tougher, and in many ways more pressing, plight of poorly governed states.

In March 2002, the administration proposed a new foreign aid program called the Millennium Challenge Accounts (MCA). This is an incentive-based approach to foreign aid: make sure that aid is used effectively by giving it only to governments that can demonstrate a record of good governance. What such a record requires is "ruling justly" (promoting human rights and democratization), "investing in people" (education and health care), and "pursuing sound economic policies" (enhancing opportunities for economic well-being). This may sound like a reasonable, even enlightened, policy. In practice, however, it means that these new funds will be targeted at the countries that are most likely to succeed without them. It ignores the real problem: how to deal with badly governed countries, the weak states least likely to develop economically, most likely to have high rates of human rights abuses, and most attractive to transnational criminal networks and terrorist organizations. The MCA does solve some problems of existing U.S. foreign aid, but it does this by picking winners and ignoring losers.

Responding to Past Complaints

The MCA was designed to address a number of criticisms of existing foreign aid programs: In response to the complaint that U.S. aid is inadequate, it proposes a 50 percent increase. This is all new money, rather than a re-allocation of funds from elsewhere in the foreign aid budget. The additional cash will still leave the United States last among the twenty-two Organization for Economic Cooperation and Development (OECD) countries in foreign aid as a percentage of gross national product [GNP], although we may now give Italy some serious competition for twenty-first place. Like most of the OECD countries, the United States will remain far below its commitment to give .7 percent of GNP in aid, made in the Agenda 21 agreement at the Earth Summit in 1992. It will, however, firmly establish the United States as the largest single giver of aid. That honor had been held by Japan until 2001. The change was due, first, to the weakening value of the yen and then to increased U.S. aid connected to the war on terrorism, including a $600 million package given to Pakistan as a reward for its support in Afghanistan.

In response to the complaint that U.S. aid is manipulated for political purposes, MCA country eligibility is to be determined by "objective and quantifiable" criteria, according to the authorizing legislation. Data will be drawn from various publicly available sources, including the World Bank, Freedom House, the World Health Organization, UNESCO [United Nations Educational, Scientific and Cultural Organization], the Heritage Foundation, and commercial credit rating services. All the data are available on the Internet, and so the process of identifying eligible countries should be completely transparent. In addition, MCA funds are to be used exclusively for economic development. No money will be given for military aid.

Traditionally most U.S. aid was given in the form of loans rather than grants. This can create a debt burden for countries that fail to use aid effectively, whether because of poor governance or bad luck. Despite concessionary rates of interest, the practice of using loans has also generated complaints that aid is designed to make recipient countries more dependent on donors. The MCA addresses this criticism by using grants rather than loans. However, this does not represent a dramatic break with current policy. Since the 1970s the proportion of grants to loans in U.S. economic assistance programs has been growing, and grants already represent the lion's share of foreign aid.

A Corporate Structure

Some Americans have complained that the U.S. Agency for International Development [USAID], which disburses the bulk of traditional foreign aid, is an inefficient, bloated bureaucracy that attempts to micromanage aid projects. USAID does closely monitor aid use and disbursement, in part because a great deal of money has been embezzled or misused by recipient governments in the past, and the monitoring requires a large staff. MCA funds will be administered instead by a Millennium Challenge Corporation [MCC]. It is unclear what difference this corporate structure will make: the CEO [chief executive officer] of the corporation will be chosen by and accountable to a board of directors chaired by the secretary of state. Other board members will include the secretary of the treasury, the U.S. trade representative, the administrator of USAID, and four presidential appointees. As with USAID, Congress will appropriate the MCC's budget, and will thus be able to place significant constraints on the organization. The board may create greater transparency, but it is unclear that it will create greater efficiency. The administration has planned for a staff of 100–200 to manage an estimated five billion dollars, one-third of the foreign aid budget. As of July 2004, only forty people had been hired, despite the fact that the process of soliciting proposals is well underway. Even if it is able to manage the granting process, this small staff won't be able to monitor the use of grant funds. At a minimum, significant outsourcing of oversight will be required. . . .

Table 1. MCA Eligible Countries and Worst-Governed States Compared

		Government Effectiveness	Political Terror	Political Rights	HDI
Worst-Governed States	Afghanistan	-1.39	5	1	NA
	Burma	-1.29	3	1	0.55
	Burundi	-1.46	5	2	0.34
	Central African Rep.	-1.43	3	3	0.36
	Congo - Kinshasa	-1.60	5	2	0.35
	Equatorial Guinea	-1.37	3	2	0.66
	Guinea - Bissau	-1.35	2	4	0.37
	Haiti	-1.56	3	2	0.47
	Iraq	-1.64	4	1	0.58
	Liberia	-1.51	5	2	NA
	North Korea	-1.78	3	1	NA
	Paraguay	-1.29	2	4	0.75
	Sierra Leone	-1.54	2	4	0.28
	Solomon Islands	-1.34	3	4	0.63
	Somalia	-1.97	4	2	0.28
	Turkmenistan	-1.47	2	1	0.75
	Average	**-1.51**	**3.47**	**2.13**	**0.49**
MCA Candidates	Armenia	-0.42	2	4	0.73
	Benin	-0.62	2	5	0.41
	Bolivia	-0.53	2	7	0.67
	Cape Verde	-0.20	2	7	0.73
	Georgia	-0.77	2	4	0.75
	Ghana	-0.01	2	6	0.57
	Honduras	-0.73	3	5	0.67
	Lesotho	-0.26	2	4	0.51
	Madagascar	-0.38	3	6	0.47
	Mali	-0.84	1	6	0.34
	Mongolia	-0.18	1	6	0.66
	Mozambique	-0.41	2	5	0.36
	Nicaragua	-0.87	2	5	0.64
	Senegal	-0.18	2	5	0.43
	Sri Lanka	-0.03	3	5	0.73
	Vanuatu	-0.64	2	7	0.57
	Average	**-0.44**	**2.06**	**5.44**	**0.58**
		Scores vary ±2.5 with a mean of 1	Scale from 1 (best) to 5 (worst) with a mean of 3.29	Scale from 1 (worst) to 7 (best) with a mean of 4.55	Scores vary from 0 (worst) to 1 (best) with a mean of 0.7

SOURCES: Radelet, "Qualifying for the Millennium Challenge Account" (MCA candidates), Purdue PTS (PTS [AI]), Freedom House (Political Rights), UNDP *Human Development Report* (HDI), Kaufman, Kraay, and Mastruzzi, "Governance Matters III" (Government Effectiveness). Data are for 2002 where available, or for the nearest available year.

Helping Nations That Are Already Bound to Succeed

Qualifying for the MCA requires states to document a record of good governance. Eligibility is competitive: countries will need to exceed the mean score for their peer group to qualify, the peer groups being set by gross domestic product per capita cutoff points (less than $1,435/year in 2004). Continued grants depend on continued high performance. If successful, the program could provide incentives to improve governance in qualifying countries, and in countries that come very close to qualifying. The improvements could include controlling corruption, developing expertise for competent economic planning, permitting the full exercise of civil and political rights, educating citizens, providing health care, and ensuring security for people and property.

However, the emphasis on good governance means that the benefits of the program will go to countries that already enjoy a high level of state capacity. By design the program selects the best-governed low-income countries. Yet these are the countries that are already best off and most likely to succeed. Indeed, they are the countries that are already most likely to use aid effectively and therefore are in the best position to pay off traditional development loans.

The countries that do not qualify, and are not likely ever to qualify, are the ones that are worst governed—and those are the countries that have the most severe problems with poverty, lack of education, poor health care, human rights abuse, and political instability. Table 1 compares the sixteen worst-governed states in the world, according to the World Bank's measure of "government effectiveness," with the sixteen countries eligible in the program's first year. None of the worst-governed countries will qualify for the MCA. They are the states with the worst records of human rights abuse, as measured by the Political Terror scale, a five-point scale derived from Amnesty International reports. Five is the worst score on the Political Terror scale. The MCA countries average 2.06, while the worst-governed states average 3.38. Much the same is true for political rights, measured using the seven-point Freedom House scale: MCA candidates are already likely to be more democratic. The scale is inverted here, so that a seven indicates the highest level of political rights, while a one indicates the lowest. The worst-governed states average 2.25. The MCA candidates average 5.44, and none receives a score below 4.

Finally, the worst-governed states stand at a much lower level on the UN Development Program's composite indicator of economic well-being, the Human Development Index (HDI). This compares countries on the basis of literacy rates, life expectancy, and GDP [gross domestic product] per capita, with a measure ranging from one to zero (in practice, the minimum value is .28—a tie between Sierra Leone and Somalia). The worst-governed states average .49 on the HDI, although their score would probably be lower if data were available for all fifteen countries: it is only the relatively better of the worst-governed states that can collect the information that goes into the HDI calculation. The MCA countries average .58. Fully four of them are above the global mean of .70.

No Help for the Most Troubled Nations

Thus, the sixteen states that qualify for the first year of the program not only have better governance, they are also ahead with regard to human rights, political openness, and economic well-being. This discrepancy is not surprising, because the MCA criteria are designed to select precisely such states. But this is the great shortcoming of the program. It is unlikely that the MCA will prevent state collapse, safeguard rights, or improve the standard of living in the worst states. Nor are the worst states likely to improve much on their own, if the conventional economic theory is correct: that competent, effective, and honest bureaucracies are necessary for economic growth. States will not grow by themselves into MCA-qualifying status: they must be helped. At its May 2004 board meeting, the MCC voted to develop a "threshold country" program to improve governance in states that come very close to meeting the MCA criteria. But this still avoids the question of how to help the states in deepest trouble.

The MCA is not a program to assist states to develop better governance. Nor is there any such program in the traditional USAID repertoire. The closest existing program is the Peace Corps, which has the goal of raising educational standards and skill levels in developing countries, and is incidentally the aid program that is most effective at building goodwill for the United States. Without a program to build state capacity, the worst-off states won't improve on their own.

An addendum to the MCA is needed to assist weak and poorly governed states in developing sufficient state capacity to aspire to be MCA candidates. This would extend the logic of the MCA's incentive-based approach to the most poorly-performing countries. It would give them reasons to reform, which they will never have if they feel permanently cut out of the program. And the governments of these states are likely to welcome assistance framed in terms of improving state capacity to perform routine, system-maintaining tasks—tax collection, law and order, and the extension of central control over regional petty despots.

There are multiple reasons to give foreign aid. There is an ethical interest in reducing poverty, a security interest in creating goodwill and stability, and an economic interest in creating foreign markets for U.S. goods. By targeting the countries most likely to succeed, the MCA maximizes the probability of achieving the last objective. But it mostly neglects the first two. The MCA picks countries that are already winners so as to maximize the probability that they will contribute to the global economy, and by extension the U.S. economy. By picking well-governed countries, it ignores weak states. By picking

democracies, it ignores human rights abuse. By picking countries with good educational and health services, it ignores
misery and ignorance. The MCA leaves behind the most dis-
advantaged people in global society. To help those people, we
need to add programs specifically designed to address their
problems, which are, politically and economically, the hardest
problems, and which the administration's new aid policy does
not even acknowledge.

> *"The United States has a moral imperative to advocate that individuals around the world have the freedom to pursue their dreams in a secure, prosperous and peaceful environment."*

The United States Promotes Democracy in the Third World

Paula J. Dobriansky

In the following viewpoint the U.S. undersecretary of state for global affairs, Paula J. Dobriansky, argues that the United States has a "moral imperative" to assist nations worldwide in establishing democratic rule. Dobriansky maintains that U.S. efforts at exporting democracy include participating in leagues of countries interested in pursuing good governance, and proffering aid packages to governments that have shown an inclination toward the rule of law and social responsibility. She insists that through such efforts, the United States can vanquish despotism around the world and bring development and stability to struggling nations.

As you read, consider the following questions:

1. In Dobriansky's view, how does promoting democracy aid the war on terrorism?

Paula J. Dobriansky, "Advancing Democracy," *National Interest,* Fall 2004, pp. 71–78. Copyright © 2004 by *National Interest.* Reproduced by permission.

2. According to the author, what significance did Francisco Flores's speech have for nations assembled at the Community of Democracies meeting in June 2003?

3. What kinds of projects does Dobriansky say are financed by the Human Rights and Democracy Fund?

I n the Summer 2004 issue of *The National Interest,* Adrian Karatnycky called for "an effort to press democracy's expansion" that would take advantage of what he described as

an opening in history when there is a chance utterly to vanquish and banish the worst forms of tyranny and autocracy and replace them with an order rooted in the rule of law and democratic accountability before the people.

He is correct that the end of the Cold War and the attendant U.S.-Soviet nuclear stand-off have created a geostrategic landscape in which there is an unprecedented opportunity for the promotion of democracy. In fact, the United States is already pursuing this course. As President [George W.] Bush stated in his introduction to the National Security Strategy released in 2002, America seeks "to create a balance of power that favors human freedom" and "will actively work to bring the hope of democracy, development, free markets, and free trade to every corner of the world."

A U.S. Imperative

President Bush is committed to these objectives because they are the right thing to do: The advent of democracy—backed up by the rule of law, limited government and civil society—advances human freedom and human dignity while empowering individuals and societies to reach their greatest potential.

The United States has a moral imperative to advocate that individuals around the world have the freedom to pursue their dreams in a secure, prosperous and peaceful environment. Promoting democracy also advances other important interests worldwide. Most immediately, it is an indispensable component of any viable strategy for winning the global war against terrorism, which poses a grave threat to international security in the 21st century. Democracy facilitates the establishment of legitimate and law-based political systems in states that may become sponsors or havens for terrorists, creates peaceful channels to reconcile grievances that can otherwise fuel bloody and destabilizing conflicts within nations, and instills hope, replacing the sense of powerlessness and despair that sometimes transforms ordinary people into willing terrorist recruits. It can also contribute to broader prosperity, which enhances stability and creates opportunities to expand trade and investment ties between nations.

Democracy-building is a protracted process, and one or two free elections do not a democracy make. A mature democracy requires far more than periodic holding of even free and fair elections. It calls for limited government, with many of the economic, social and cultural issues being handled within a private sphere. The rule of law is another must, with a particular emphasis on ensuring governmental accountability. Even though building a mature democracy may take a long time, we should pursue such a goal with vigor and dispatch.

While we believe that our constitutional structure and political philosophy contain unique insights into how to build and manage a multi-ethnic and diverse democracy, and while we are happy to share our experience, promoting democracy does not mean imposing the American political and constitutional model on other countries. On the contrary, citizens in emerging democracies must be free to develop institutions compatible with their own cultures and experiences. The desire for freedom, the rule of law and a vibrant civil society, and for a voice in one's government, is universal, but the specific institutional expressions of democracy will naturally vary by country.

The Significance of Democracy in Developing Countries

Democracy . . . offers a better way for developing countries to deal with . . . obstacles to holistic development. Through open discourse and political activity, it provides peaceful and more effective means for diverse groups within developing countries to negotiate answers to ethnic and regional cleavages, interest-group conflicts, and ideological differences. For instance, the late Costa Rican intellectual Luis Burstin suggest[ed] that revolutions in Latin America have been provoked not by poverty and social injustice but by rigid, undemocratic systems that block access to political power for emerging groups.

Democratic institutions thus provide constitutional, nonviolent alternatives that are otherwise absent in undemocratic states. This forestalls the buildup of dangerous tensions, which can erupt in sectarian violence as in Rwanda, Indonesia, Sri Lanka, and numerous other places. Because political and societal stability impacts a developing country's economic attractiveness, the absence of an open, participatory political system is, in fact, an obstacle to development.

Yu-Ping Chan, Harvard International Review, *Fall 2001.*

Blueprint for Good Governance

Under this administration, U.S. efforts to promote democracy have taken several forms. Indeed, they have been as comprehensive and varied as the numerous challenges involved in democratization. One of our most exciting—and perhaps lesser known—endeavors is the Community of Democracies (CD), an unprecedented network of over 130 established and emerging democratic countries committed to strengthening democratic institutions and spreading democratic values worldwide. At its founding meeting in Warsaw in June 2000, an extraordinary group of ministers affirmed these principles in the Warsaw Declaration. Two years later, at the subsequent Ministerial Conference in Seoul in November 2002, the CD moved from affirmation to action, devising an ambitious and practical blueprint for its work. Known as the Seoul Plan of Action, this document spells out concrete areas for cooperative action among the participants, ranging from developing regional human rights and democracy-monitoring mechanisms, to promoting good governance practices and responding to threats to democracy.

Some recent activities of the Community of Democracies illustrate its practical approach and underscore its tremendous potential and growing impact. In June 2003, for example, government officials and NGO [nongovernmental organization] leaders from 14 African, Latin American and Caribbean democracies, as well as representatives of the African Union, the Organization of American States (OAS), and other regional organizations, met in Miami to discuss how they could most effectively address local threats to democratic governance. One of the most compelling moments during this gathering was a ten-minute speech by El Salvador's then-president, Francisco Flores, who movingly enumerated his country's enormous achievements during the last 15 years and described them as

> eloquent proof that El Salvador has discovered the path to defeat poverty and to attain prosperity. This path is called democracy, and it is based on this essential concept: that Salvadorans know how to resolve their problems; they just needed a chance to do it.

It is one thing for American officials to deliver this message, as we often do, but it is something else entirely for leaders in developing democracies to hear it from their peers. This discussion has intensified in the Western Hemisphere, where leaders of OAS member states participating in the special Summit of the Americas in Monterrey, Mexico, earlier this year [2004] explicitly recognized the Community of Democracies' work and urged the body to continue its efforts to strengthen democratic institutions. . . .

These efforts are already bearing fruit. During the annual session of the UN Commission on Human Rights earlier this year, members of the CD's Convening Group and other democracies joined forces to support a resolution emphasizing the importance of good governance in protecting and promoting human rights. This group also backed resolutions on the incompatibility of democracy and racism and the need to strengthen the role of regional organizations in promoting democracy. Although many governments regularly support their neighbors (or avoid antagonizing them) and align along socioeconomic lines, the emerging democracy caucus has established a complementary mechanism that, while respecting existing institutions, can also advance democratic values as a basis for cooperative action. Increasing coordination among democracies—and persuading them to vote together as democracies—can make a difference.

Disbursing Aid to Nations Demonstrating Good Governance

The recent establishment of the Millennium Challenge Account (MCA) is another creative American policy that will contribute to the expansion of democracy. Announced [in 2002] by President Bush, this innovative initiative rewards developing nations that "make the right [governance] choices"— measured by their performance on 16 indicators—by offering the opportunity for additional U.S. assistance. Congress authorized $1 billion for this purpose in 2004; the president has requested $2.5 billion for 2005 and is committed to seeking $5 billion for 2006. Full funding for the MCA would mean adding 50 percent to the $10 billion that America provided through core development programs when the program was announced in 2002. In May 2004 the Board of Directors of the Millennium Challenge Corporation—the implementing organization, chaired by Secretary of State Colin Powell—announced a list of the first 16 countries eligible to apply for these funds.

The core logic of our approach is that, in the absence of political will to advance proven political and economic approaches, traditional development assistance cannot produce sustained progress on its own. Providing assistance without a strong commitment by the receiving government to improve citizen's lives is often unproductive, if not counterproductive, by helping leaders to continue business as usual. This situation has led some critics to question the value of foreign aid. However, from the very beginning, the Bush Administration has maintained that we need to reform the way development assistance is provided, focusing new attention on lasting development progress through partnership and mutual effort. The MCA builds on fifty years of experience by supporting those governments that have already demonstrated a commitment in three crucial areas: governing justly, investing in their people and encouraging economic freedom. Helping countries that have good laws and effective and transparent policies makes sense; they are best able to take advantage of U.S. assistance and, eventually, should no longer need it. . . .

Other Forms of Democratic Assistance

Needless to say, the United States also provides financial support to projects around the world that advance the development of civil society, free media and political parties and that promote human rights. The Department of State provides assistance directly through grants from programs like its Human Rights and Democracy Fund, which has more than tripled in size between 2001 and 2004, rising to $43 million. These funds go to important grassroots projects, such as legal assistance and human rights education in Uzbekistan, NGO development in China and the only independent radio station in Angola.

The Agency for International Development works to advance democracy as well through its Democracy and Governance programs, which focus on the four key areas of the rule of law, elections and political processes, civil society and governance.

Finally, the U.S. government works closely with a variety of domestic and international non-governmental organizations, such as the National Endowment for Democracy, the International Foundation for Electoral Systems and the Council for a Community of Democracies, among others. These groups are vital partners, contributing enormously to worldwide efforts to promote democracy and human rights.

| "*Rather than promoting freedom throughout the world, the US has carried out a comprehensive program of state terrorism.*"

The United States Does Not Promote Democracy in the Third World

John S. Sorenson

John S. Sorenson is a professor of sociology at Brock University in Ontario, Canada. In the following viewpoint Sorenson rebuts the notion that the United States is the benevolent dispenser of democracy to developing nations. Sorenson insists instead that America has a history of imperialist aggression and has conducted many overt and covert operations abroad that have thwarted democratic revolutions and kept tyrants in power in the name of defending U.S. interests. These interests, Sorenson contends, are mainly those of the wealthy business conglomerates who gain an advantage by stalling democracy in the Third World where labor is cheap and exploitable.

As you read, consider the following questions:

1. According to Sorenson, what was the motivation behind U.S. "interventions" in foreign countries after World War II?

2. In the author's view, why would the U.S. government find it desirable to pit itself against "an evil enemy?"

3. As Sorenson reports it, who organized the 1954 coup that overthrew the government of Jacobo Arbenz in Guatamala?

Among the after-effects of the September 11th terrorist attacks on the World Trade Center and the Pentagon was the constraint on dissent and the characterization of opposition to the bombing of innocent civilians in Afghanistan as "anti-Americanism." A prime example is the reaction to an October 2001 speech by University of British Columbia professor Sunera Thobani at a conference in Ottawa. Corporate media seized on her characterization of US policy as "soaked in blood" and presented her as a heartless ideologue and hatemonger. A *Globe and Mail* editorial denounced her "poisonous diatribe" as "just another chance to berate the Americans," while *Globe* columnist Margaret Wente described Thobani as "an idiot." Just as charges of "anti-Semitism" are often used in an opportunistic and cynical way to undermine valid criticisms of Israeli policies, so does the term "anti-Americanism" serve to discredit critical thinking about the role of the US in a global culture of prejudice.

A Long History of Terrorism

Understanding the steady decline of social and political conditions in the Third World since the end of World War II requires discussion of US imperialism. The US is often presented as a guardian of freedom and democracy. This ignores a long history of terrorism that begins with efforts to exterminate the indigenous population, includes the enslavement of millions of Africans, and continues through international military intervention and subversion. Since 1945, the US has pursued a program for global control, not freedom. Global domination was presented as a fight against communism, a struggle between forces of good and evil, and the US military was built up on the basis of deliberately exaggerated estimates of Soviet strength. Despite its rhetoric, the Soviet Union was anti-socialist and extremely repressive, as amply demonstrated by executions, deportations, concentration camps, starvation, persecution, military interventions in East Europe, invasion of Afghanistan, and support for Third World dictatorships such as the Mengistu regime in Ethiopia. Before its eventual collapse in the 1980s, the Soviet Union's interventions were more limited in scope than those of the US.

From 1945 to the mid-1990s, the US military was deployed beyond its borders over 200 times. This included large-scale wars in Korea and Indochina along with various small wars and counter-insurgency operations in Central America, Africa, Asia, and the Middle East. US plans for post-war world order were laid out in 1950s *National Security Council Memorandum 68*, which Noam Chomsky describes as a key planning document of the US government, outlining two major post-war policies: to destroy the Soviet system and to create a global environment in which the US would preserve its wealth and power. In 1948 George Kennan, State Department Director of Policy Planning, noted,

> We have 50% of the world's wealth but only 6.3% of its population. In this situation we cannot fail to be the object of envy and resentment. Our real task in the coming period is to devise a pattern of relationships which will allow us to maintain this position of disparity.... We should cease to talk about the raising of the living standards, human rights and democratization. The day is not far off when we are going to have to deal in straight power concepts. The less we are then hampered by idealistic slogans, the better.

To a large extent, the US has been able to maintain this division of wealth. In 1992, the United Nations found 83 per cent of the world's wealth concentrated in the North [i.e., in the northern hemisphere], benefitting 20 per cent of the world's population. The gap between rich and poor is growing: in 1960, the wealthiest nations were 30 times richer than the poorest; in 1990 they were 60 times richer. Distribution of wealth within countries shows the richest 20 per cent of the world's people are 150 times richer than the poorest 20 per cent.

Emphasizing the Soviet Threat

US planners exaggerated Soviet threats as a means to mobilize support for intervention in the Third World and to justify murder, torture, and repression. They warned that communism would find a receptive audience in the Third World so the US had to intervene aggressively. While claiming to act in the interests of freedom and democracy, the US tried to *prevent* democracy in the Third World, as well as at home.

Military spending was considered the key to US economic development, but it was necessary to convince the population to support military budgets and cut social spending. A standard propaganda device to mobilize reluctant populations is the threat of an evil enemy. The Soviet threat was used to gain support for unpopular policies of increased military spending and to justify internal repression in the US. Corporate-funded anti-communist propaganda helped to weaken the labour movement and strengthen the power of business. The Soviet threat also was used to build an industrial system based on military production, which helped to secure corporate power and establish a world order in the interests of US corporations.

The real Soviet threat was not its inferior military capacity, but its ideological challenge to US domination. For its own purposes, the Soviet Union supported states like Cuba and Nicaragua that tried to avoid total US domination and blocked full exploitation of areas intended to provide raw materials, markets, and cheap labour. To crush such threats, the US supported military regimes in the Third World, training tens of

Backlash Against U.S.-Imposed Democracy

Some African states are perilously close to civil wars as a result of anti-democratic executive behavior. . . . There are countries around the world where the imposition of Western-style democracy may either precipitate unwelcome consequences for the societies in question, or result in the growth of powerful, authoritarian executive governments as "keepers of the democratic order." While President George W. Bush's policy of spreading and aiding the development of democracy abroad certainly carries long-term benefits to the United States and the West as a whole, it is important to remember that not all societies where democracy is imposed or influenced by the U.S. are countries where peace, stability and respect for human rights necessarily prevail.

Yevgeny Bendersky, Power and Interest News Report, *February 23, 2005.*

thousands of Third World military and police officers in its School of the Americas, where they were indoctrinated in capitalist ideology and trained to use torture and [to] terrorize civilian populations. . . .

A World to Suit US Interests

The US emerged from World War II with unprecedented economic and military power and set about designing a global system to suit US interests, that is, those of business elites.

The US intervened in various countries to achieve its goals. . . .

The US helped to overthrow Iran's parliamentary system in 1953 and reestablished dictatorship under the Shah, hoping to gain control of vast oil reserves. After the CIA backed the Shah's coup, US companies obtained 40 per cent of oil concessions (previously controlled by Britain). Extremely corrupt, the Shah used US power to obtain his goals, and ruled through repression. SAVAK, the secret police created and trained by the CIA and Israel's MOSSAD covert operations unit, used torture regularly. Repression under the Shah and US support for torture and murder encouraged Iranians to regard Western lifestyles as corrupt and contributed to the eventual rise of Islamic fundamentalism.

Intervention in the Philippines is rooted in US colonization in the nineteenth century. Thousands were slaughtered in a brutal war directed against the civilian population by the same US troops that had recently been used to exterminate much of the indigenous population of North America; the same racist ideology fuelled both genocidal efforts. US colonization lasted until 1946, despite a brief Japanese occupation, and the economy was dominated by the US and a small, local land-owning elite. When the Philippines received nominal independence, the Communist Party, which had led anti-Japanese forces during World War II, was suppressed with US assistance. Ferdinand Marcos, who became president in 1965, was one of the Third World's most corrupt leaders, transferring huge amounts of public funds into his own accounts and those of family and friends, while transforming the military into his personal army. While Marcos and his friends enjoyed fabulous wealth, most of the population were desperately poor, without health care, education or housing. Cheap labour and generous tax breaks for foreign investment allowed US corporations to operate with extremely low costs. Expansion of export-oriented agriculture dispossessed the peasants, rendering the majority landless, created deforestation, reduced food production for local consumption, and resulted in widespread disease and malnutrition. Opposition was repressed through extensive human rights violations, including torture and assassination by the US trained police and military. Although an earlier peasant-based guerrilla insurgency in the 1950s was smashed with US military aid, advisors, and counter-insurgency operations, the New People's Army launched a guerrilla war. Again the US helped the military to crush the opposition that had spread through most levels of society; this opposition had taken an anti-US character because the US had supported Marcos' depredations to achieve its own interests. . . . The US wanted to use Marcos as a puppet but found it hard to control his greed. This avarice created strong opposition, and eventually the US tried to distance itself from him. Although Marcos was eventually deposed in 1986, guerrilla war did not end and US military aid continued under Corazon Aquino. CIA involvement in counter-insurgency increased, helped by fanatical right-wing Christian fundamentalist groups who encourage vigilante death squads to kill communists, union activists, and more liberal religious leaders. Opposition continues because the conditions that created it, the desperately poor situation of the majority of the population, have not changed.

US Actions in Latin America

In Latin America, the US has substantial economic interests that it does not want threatened by nationalism or calls for social justice. US planners saw the military as an ally and removed other leaders who interfered with US business interests. For example, in Guatemala the CIA organized a 1954 coup to depose the government of Jacobo Arbenz, who had been reluctant to grant oil concessions to US companies and introduced land reform that affected the giant United Fruit Corporation. Arbenz wanted United Fruit to improve conditions by paying a minimum wage that would allow workers to avoid malnutrition and starvation. The government also expropriated unused land of United Fruit and gave it to peasants so they could feed themselves, and offered to pay compensation to the corporation. United Fruit, with close links to the US government, lobbied for the overthrow of Arbenz, pointing out that agrarian reform was a dangerous threat that might appeal to workers and peasants elsewhere who were similarly oppressed by local ruling classes and US corporations and who might aspire to a minimum standard of living. The US government and United Fruit cooperated in a massive propaganda campaign, warning that Guatemala had been taken over by communists and that a serious threat from the Soviet Union existed. The US supported military officers connected to Guatemala's oligarchy who were unhappy about land reform. The coup restored United Fruit's land and reversed social reform, dismantling co-ops and literacy programs. Thousands of Guatemalans—teachers, unionists, students, and peasants—disappeared or were arrested or murdered. The pattern continued: death squads, massacres, and torture designed to terrorize the population and keep them in squalor while large land-owners and US corporations profited. For decades, the US continued to support a series of brutal dictators in Guatemala.

The development model imposed on Guatemala was much the same as elsewhere in Latin America: a focus on cattle and agricultural products for export. The results of development included extensive deforestation, destruction of subsistence agriculture, impoverishment of most of the population, hunger, malnutrition, generalized misery and fear, pesticide poisoning, genocidal attacks on villages that might provide assistance to anti-government guerrillas (themselves created by these conditions) with over 100,000 killed, thousands missing, forced relocation, mass refugee movements, slavery, and child prostitution. Such conditions offered US corporations a good climate for business: workers earned a few dollars for a sixteen hour day in appalling conditions and union organizers were murdered. Eventually, global recession, falling prices, rising inflation and unemployment, and high military spending created economic disaster and convinced the junta to allow a civilian government to take over, although they would still control it and block investigation of human rights violations.

Supporting State Terrorism

These few examples are part of a much longer record of US brutality. Seeking hegemony in Asia in the 1960s, the US destroyed Vietnam, Laos, and Cambodia through saturation bombing. In Chile, a CIA-directed coup deposed the elected Allende government and resulted in the deaths of thousands. The US provided lists of "communists" (a conveniently all-inclusive term) for the Indonesian military junta, who killed up to a million people in 1965, and supported the same murderers in their genocidal attack on East Timor. The US supported death squads in El Salvador and supplied the terrorist Contra guerrillas in their efforts to overthrow the Sandinista government of Nicaragua. The US has supported fascist regimes around the world, backed the apartheid state in South Africa, supported Israel's invasion of Lebanon and its ongoing occupation of Palestine, and maintained its long and destructive embargo on Cuba. The US has invaded or bombed countries such as Grenada, Haiti, Libya, Panama and Sudan. The bombing of Iraq and sanctions against that country have killed up to a million people. The US provides major support to the governments of Colombia and Turkey, both of which have terrorized and attacked their own populations. These cases demonstrate how the US government has used violence and terrorism to maintain the structural inequalities of global capitalism.

Rather than promoting freedom throughout the world, the US has carried out a comprehensive program of state terrorism through officially declared wars and through counter-insurgency operations. It has attacked civilian populations, deposed governments, and created and maintained some of the world's most vicious dictatorships. These activities have helped to create a globalized culture of prejudice in which the bulk of the world's population is denied even their most basic needs while a small elite enjoys fantastic wealth and power. Those who applaud the USA as a defender of global freedom should bear in mind these historical realities. To point them out is neither to engage in "anti-Americanism" nor to ignore the brutality of other states, but merely to recognize that all states serve the interests of the rich and the powerful and that the US is dedicated to serving these interests on a global scale.

The campaign to dismiss critical analysis as "anti-Americanism" demonstrates the ubiquity of hegemonic power in the culture of prejudice and the ability to redefine historical and political realities. The actual record of violence and terrorism conducted in the service of US business interests and strategic goals is seldom allowed to intrude upon the picture of altruism and saintly beneficence that is constructed in corporate media and in the statements of business and political leaders. Since September 11, 2001, the US has been portrayed as the innocent victim of international terrorism rather than as its main perpetrator and sponsor. The atrocities of US imperialism are ignored and even the term "imperialism" itself rarely figures. When it does, it is immediately rejected. For example, columnist Margaret Wente dismisses charges of imperialism as a mistaken notion of a foolish intelligentsia as she praises President George W. Bush (and by extension the US): "Actually he's not an imperialist. He's a genuine idealist, who wants to spread democracy and freedom because he thinks those things will make people happier and better off and the US more secure." While dissident voices are not completely banned, the corporate control of mass media ensures that they are marginalized. The power of corporate media ensures the dissemination of propaganda that portrays the US as the sentinel of freedom. It is the role of critical scholars to challenge these hegemonic depictions and the apologists for imperialism and international terrorism.

| "U.S. assistance [to Africa] increased from $10 billion in 2000 to $19 billion in 2004."

U.S. Aid to Africa Is Increasing

Andrew Natsios

Andrew Natsios is the administrator of the United States Agency for International Development (USAID). In the following viewpoint, a speech he gave in 2005 at the United Nations Dialogue on Financing for Development, Natsios maintains that the United States is committed to supplying African nations with aid. According to Natsios, the U.S. government has already surpassed its decreed aid pledges and is now responsible for a quarter of the assistance pledged by the twenty-one nations in the Organization for Economic Cooperation and Development (OECD).

As you read, consider the following questions:

1. According to Natsios, what four concepts are African leaders "linking" in their support for development?
2. About how much does the author say the United States contributed to the Global Fund to fight AIDS in 2004?
3. In Natsios's view, why is developing private markets "indispensable" for developing countries?

Andrew Natsios, statement at the United Nations High Level Dialogue on Financing for Development, New York, June 27, 2005.

T oday [June 2005], three years after the U.N. Conference on Financing for Development, its outcome—the Monterrey Consensus [in which attending developing nations agreed that good governance should be a determining factor for receiving aid]—has become the definitive framework for successful development. Developing countries and donors alike have embraced its emphasis on good governance and domestic ownership of development strategies, while trade and private investment are widely recognized as essential.

In setting out the principles of the New Partnership for African Development (NEPAD), African leaders are linking poverty eradication, sustainable growth, global integration, and good governance. We, in the United States, are enthusiastic about NEPAD and are providing support to the initiative.

For its part, the United States has increased Official Development Assistance [ODA] even beyond President [George W.] Bush's Monterrey pledge—U.S. assistance increased from $10 billion in 2000 to $19 billion in 2004—a quarter of the Organization for Economic Cooperation and Development [OECD] total.

However, these ODA increases must be matched by increases in effectiveness and sustainability. Achieving the goals of the Millennium Declaration [a UN plan that set goals for the worldwide reduction of poverty, hunger, and other social ills] is not just about the mobilization of resources alone.

Countries that have proven their commitment to change and reform—that govern justly, invest in their people and maintain policies and institutions that support market-led growth—will receive billions of dollars from the Millennium Challenge Corporation [the U.S. organization responsible for delivering aid to developing nations that show an inclination toward good governance] of the United States Government in coming years.

Too often, humanitarian relief has been separated from development and from achievement of the goals of the Mil-

A Commitment to African Development

Sub-Saharan Africa posted its strongest level of overall GDP [gross domestic product] growth in eight years in 2004, topping 5 percent. Mozambique, Tanzania, and Senegal are among countries with robust growth rates. However, in 2003, average GDP per capita in Africa was still only $500, less than one-tenth the global average of $5,510.

The United States encourages national efforts to promote private-sector-led growth, develop trade, and build skills, markets, and private sector institutions. By the end of 2003, the U.S. direct investment position had increased 18.7 percent from 2002 levels to $11.5 billion. The U.S. government has forged alliances with European and American companies to create jobs and raise incomes in Africa and to increase African exports.

U.S. Agency for International Development,
Building on Africa's Promise, June 2005.

lennium Declaration, as though they are not related to each other. In Africa—which has more fragile or vulnerable states than any other region—we must respond to the current food emergency or these countries will be destined for further instability and the achievement of their development goals will be even more difficult.

Humanitarian Efforts

To assist states in crisis and conflict [to] return to stability and get on the path to sustained growth, President Bush recently announced that we will provide an additional $674 million for humanitarian emergencies in Africa [in 2005] in partnership with the United Kingdom—beyond the approximately $1.4 billion already committed.

By joining with socially responsible private sector partners in our Global Development Alliance, United States Agency for International Development [USAID] since 2002 has invested $1 billion in 290 public-private alliances in 98 countries—and thus leveraged more than $3.7 billion in total partner resources.

As a founder and largest donor of the Global Fund to Fight HlV/AIDS, Tuberculosis and Malaria, the United States Government provided $459 million to the Fund in 2004. The U.S. contribution for HlV/AIDS programs totaled more than $2.8 billion in the current [2005] fiscal year. In addition, we provide approximately $500 million annually for voluntary family planning and maternal health care in 60 countries.

Without sustained high rates of economic growth in developing countries, the achievement of the goals of the Millennium Declaration will be put at risk.

The United States leads the world in liberalizing trade and helping countries participate in negotiations, obtain commitments, and benefit from trade. The completion of the Doha Round [a series of trade negotiations under the auspices of the World Trade Organization], to which the U.S. is committed, could add $200 billion annually to developing countries' income and lift more than 500 million people out of poverty.

The U.S. and other G-8 countries [a group of eight leading industrialized nations] have called for 100 percent cancellation of debt obligations owed to the World Bank, the African Development Bank, and the International Monetary Fund, which will result in approximately $40 billion in immediate debt relief—and could reach more than $56 billion if all Heavily Indebted Poor Countries become eligible.

Good Governance Guarantees

We recognize that the volumes of aid and other development resources must increase significantly. But if we are to continue the recent increases in ODA and assure the goals of the Millennium Declaration are achieved, we must also ensure aid effectiveness, sustainability and results.

There is ample evidence that ODA is not usually the limiting factor on national development. Development progress is, first and foremost, a function of country commitment and political will to rule justly, promote economic freedom and invest in people.

The Report of the U.N. Commission on the Private Sector and Development estimates that developing countries have $9.4 trillion dollars in private financial assets that cannot be fully mobilized for development, largely because of corruption and inadequate legal protections for property and contracts.

Competitive, well-regulated private markets are indispensable because they are the most effective institution ever devised for allocating resources efficiently, for fostering innovation, and for communicating information that helps consumers and producers make decisions. Regulatory frameworks should aim to build the public's confidence in private markets to protect property, enforce contracts, and generally respect the rule of law.

According to a World Bank study, in one developing country, it takes 203 days to register a business, while in yet another country, enforcing a contract takes 1,459 days. With barriers to business formation and entrepreneurship like this, businesses remain small and in the informal sector. There is no point in debating whether ODA should be $68 billion or $100 billion or $195 billion when the most basic policies for generating wealth are not in place.

A significant way that the U.N. can support development is by helping countries make and implement the right choices in governing well. The U.N. is well placed to offer such assistance, for example, through providing a forum for south-south peer reviews [i.e., peer reviews among developing nations] and showcasing progress on nations' efforts to strengthen the rule of law, govern justly, end corruption, strengthen the financial sector, attract businesses to the formal sector, and open up trade. Policy reforms such as these should be at the heart of the UN's development activities. . . .

Ending poverty is a serious challenge. Building effective and equitable economic institutions takes time, persistence, and reform. Policies must be put in place to safeguard the most vulnerable members of society. The good news is that many countries have already blazed a trail and that the United States and the international community will help those prepared to help themselves. With the right choices, we have a good chance of reaching the goals we set for ourselves at Monterrey and in the Millennium Declaration.

> "[The] claim that the world has com-
> mitted to a massive increase in new
> aid to Africa relies on a very rosy
> interpretation of U.S. spending pro-
> posals."

U.S. Aid to Africa
is Overstated

David Bryden

*In the following viewpoint, David Bryden argues that the United
States government is not significantly increasing its aid package
to Africa. According to Bryden, the George W. Bush administration is touting massive spending on African development, but
only a small portion of the aid is new money. Even with the
slight increase, Bryden asserts, the total aid falls far short of
what the United States could afford to donate. He claims that
without needed aid, medical and education programs in Africa
will continue to struggle to improve. David Bryden is the communications director of the Global AIDS Alliance, a nonprofit
organization that works to lessen the impact of AIDS on poor
countries.*

As you read, consider the following questions:

1. Why does Bryden say that the announced "doubling"
   of aid to Africa is an inaccuracy?

2. According to the author, U.S. aid to Africa is comparable to what percent of the U.S. military budget?

3. How much money is the United States expected to contribute to the Global Fund for AIDS in 2006, in Bryden's estimation? How much did the Global Fund administrators ask for?

N ow that the dust has settled from the rush of media reports about Africa brought on by the Group of Eight summit [G8, a regular meeting of eight of the most industrialized nations, including the United States], it's worth taking a closer look at what the United States has actually committed to, in terms of aid for programs to address poverty and disease in Africa.

Just prior to the Summit, President George W. Bush said he would double U.S. assistance to Africa, and announced several new programs totaling $1.65 billion. The largest component is for malaria prevention and treatment ($1.2 billion), with smaller portions for education ($400 million) and programs to combat sexual violence and abuse against women ($55 million).

Unfortunately, UK Prime Minister Tony Blair's claim that the world has committed to a massive increase in new aid to Africa relies on a very rosy interpretation of U.S. spending proposals. Make Poverty History, the UK counterpart to the U.S.-based One Campaign, correctly noted [that] less than half of the aid increase pledged by the G8 was new funding and called the G8 deal "too little and too late."

A closer look at Bush's actual spending proposal shows that only 9% of it consists of new money ($800 million of the $8.8 billion committed between 2004 and 2010). Bush did announce $674 million in what he said was "additional" spending for humanitarian emergencies in Africa, but the fine print showed this was not actually new spending. In fact, the vast majority of the so-called "doubling" of U.S. assistance Bush promised is actually funding that was slated to be provided anyway, for the most part through the Millennium Challenge Account (MCA) [a new system for disbursing aid to select nations based on their level of good governance] as well as the President's global AIDS initiative. The MCA has been notably slow-paced, and Congress may well continue denying the increases that form a large part of the Bush pledge.

Deceptive Promises

What new money there is in the U.S. proposal is primarily for programs on malaria and education. These are two areas where additional spending, directed in an effective manner, could do a great deal of good. Malaria deserves an emergency response; it is, after all, the biggest killer of African children. Between 300 and 600 million clinical cases of malaria occur each year, primarily in Africa. It has a huge economic impact on Africa, cutting the region's gross domestic product by about $12 billion annually. The disease annually kills up to 3 million people. But, while the announcement on malaria sounded big, clever use of words concealed the fact that the proposal included all funds the United States had already planned to spend.

The actual increase of $1.2 billion is significant, and is desperately needed, but $500 million of it, nearly half, would not be provided until after Bush leaves office, even though there are malaria programs that could use the full level of funding right away. Investing $3 billion a year would provide global coverage of malaria prevention and treatment, so real U.S. leadership would be providing a third of this annually, starting this year [2005].

Congress already seems prepared to act faster on malaria than the President. While for 2006, the President proposes a $30 million increase in bilateral malaria funding, this is less than the cut he had earlier proposed and less than the increase Congress is already preparing to make. In recent weeks Congress has reversed Bush's cut and approved significant increases in the account for infectious diseases, which includes

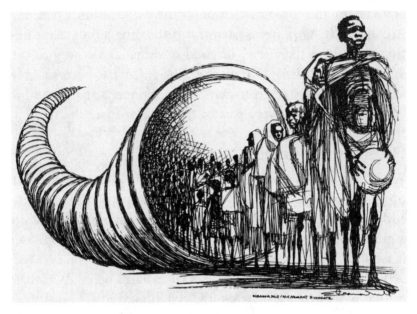

Mill © by the Mill newsart Syndicate. Reproduced by permission.

malaria funding. The House version of the foreign aid bill includes approximately $100 million for USAID [U.S. Agency for International Development] malaria programs, while the Senate version is even higher, at about $140 million.

Let's put this in perspective. The United States provides about $17.5 billion a year in foreign aid. Even though the 9/11 Commission called for increasing development assistance to safeguard global security, U.S. aid is still less than 5% of the annual military budget. Only about $6 billion of that goes toward humanitarian and development assistance. Africa receives only about 24% of all foreign aid (about $4.3 billion). Even though far richer than sub-Saharan Africa, Israel and Egypt together receive about $4.5 billion a year, more than all African countries combined.

Missed Opportunities

Just as important as the overall level of malaria funding is the way it is to be spent. The way the funds are to be channeled is highly unilateral, and this is something Congress must work to correct. Bush did not direct any of the new malaria funding to the Global Fund to Fight AIDS, Tuberculosis, and Malaria, which is the largest and most effective effort against malaria today. Louis Da Gama, the Malaria Director for the Massive Effort Campaign and a member of the Communities delegation to the Global Fund Board, was very critical of the plan. "The U.S. proposal could have had a multiplier effect if channeled through the Global Fund, since U.S. dollars would be matched two-to-one," Da Gama told journalists in a conference call. "But, sadly, the President is missing this opportunity."

The G8's declaration, which Bush signed, did mention the importance of the Global Fund. [The year 2006] is a critical year for the Fund, as its resource needs escalate. The leaders said they would "work toward" replenishment of the Fund. While Germany is notable for its low level of support for the Fund, other G8 countries, such as France and Japan, have greatly expanded their contributions for 2006 and 2007. But, while the Fund has asked the United States to provide $930 million for 2006, Bush has proposed giving just $300 million (Congressional appropriators have increased this, but only by $100 million).

The result is that while the United States claims to be the Fund's biggest supporter, at the current rate the U.S. contribution will be just 20% of all 2006 contributions. Even though France's economy is one-seventh that of the United States, the pledge from the French government is approaching what Bush has proposed the United States give in 2006, and in 2007 its contribution will exceed what Bush has proposed. . . .

Americans want to see the United States support a response to AIDS and other crises in which the United States shares the burden with other nations. This points the way to real alternatives. The United States should put much more of its funds into the Global Fund, where every dollar of the U.S. contribution is matched by two dollars from other nations. . . .

Failing Education

On education, the G8 leaders promised to support free access to primary education in Africa, but Bush's actual proposal on education fails to help eliminate school fees. The proposal's extra funding for the Africa Education Initiative will help improve educational quality, but the scholarships the Initiative provides go to only 300,000 children, instead of helping countries simply eliminate school fees altogether. Currently 25 million African children who should be in school are not attending, due to many factors including the onerous burden of school fees.

The actual funding level is extremely low, especially in the context of the quantum leap Blair and others have called for. The Commission for Africa found that up to $8 billion is needed each year to address educational inequity. Yet, Bush is proposing only to continue an existing initiative and to increase by $50 million the baseline funding level for education in Africa over the next four years. In the last four years, Congress, without significant support from the Bush administration, has increased the baseline funding level for basic education by $339 million. Therefore the supposedly new U.S. initiative represents a fraction of what Congress has already pitched in to deal with the issue.

Funding Gap

The United States also signed on to other critically important promises, such as to provide support for "all children left orphaned or vulnerable by AIDS or other pandemics" and to help countries train and retain health workers. Yet, missing from the final declaration is any mention of a process to develop a credible plan to achieve these or other critically important goals. In particular, the United States and the other

G8 countries seem to have no real strategy for how to erase the $18 billion shortfall in resources which UNAIDS [the UN's AIDS program] says countries could in fact use to fight the disease through 2007.

Progress achieved on debt cancellation could help address this funding gap. The agreement will release close to $1 billion annually in resources poor nations can use for development. Already the Zambian government has said it will use debt relief proceeds to provide AIDS drugs to 100,000 HIV/AIDS patients. But the relief of payments comes slowly, partly as a result of the difficulties countries face in meeting the economic policy conditions set by the creditors. And, while the African Union has called for all African nations to receive debt cancellation, the G-8 agreement applies to only 14.

Now, the hard work begins of pressuring leaders, including Bush and Congress, to make the actual content of U.S. proposals match the G8 summit's lofty rhetoric.

Periodical Bibliography

The following articles have been selected to supplement the diverse views presented in this chapter.

Sanjay Basu	"Dollar Diplomacy," *New Internationalist*, May 2004.
Elizabeth Becker and Richard W. Stevenson	"U.S. and Britain Agree on Relief to Poor Nations," *New York Times*, June 10, 2005.
William F. Buckley Jr.	"Trade: The Bumpy Road," *National Review*, March 28, 2005.
Alexander Cockburn	"It Should Be Late, It Was Never Great," *Nation*, December 22, 2003.
Kevin M. De Cock and Robert S. Janssen	"An Unequal Epidemic in an Unequal World," *JAMA*, July 10, 2002.
Lou Dobbs	"America the Unloved," *U.S. News & World Report*, October 13, 2003.
Jim Lacey	"We're Number Twenty?!" *National Review*, June 30, 2003.
Donald G. McNeil Jr.	"A Path to Cheaper AIDS Drugs for Poor Nations," *New York Times*, January 26, 2005.
Michael M. Phillips	"Boosting U.S. Aid to Poor Nations May Be Easier Said than Done," *Wall Street Journal*, July 15, 2002.
Gene Sperling and Tom Hart	"A Better Way to Fight Global Poverty," *Foreign Affairs*, March/April 2003.
Bruce Stokes	"Heal Thyself," *National Journal*, March 1, 2003.
James Traub	"Freedom, from Want," *New York Times Magazine*, February 13, 2005.

For Further Discussion

Chapter 1

1. How many of the Third World's problems discussed in this chapter seem to be caused or exacerbated by First World interests and policies? Cite specific examples from the viewpoints. Do you believe developed nations have a moral responsibility to solve the problems of the Third World? Why or why not? In framing your answer be sure to consider concepts such as colonialism and globalization.

2. List all of the problems facing the Third World that are discussed in this chapter. Of all the problems stalling development or negatively impacting lives, which do you think is the most salient and in need of immediate response? How will solving this chosen problem affect the solution to other problems of the Third World?

Chapter 2

1. Globalization is most often thought of as the opening up of trade between nations. As some of the authors in this chapter point out, however, the opening up of markets commonly entails the liberalizing of communication between nations. How might this latter effect of globalization better and/or worsen the lives of people in Third World nations? Use examples from the viewpoints in this chapter in your answer.

2. Authors such as Richard Sandbrook and David Romano attest that globalization divides citizens in developing nations and fosters political turmoil. List some of the ways in which these authors say that globalization can be divisive. Do you agree with these arguments? Why or why

not? If you do not agree with such arguments, suggest how globalization is being misrepresented. You may use Quan Li and Drew Schaub's viewpoint to offer counter-evidence.

3. After reading all the articles in the chapter, decide whether you think globalization is a positive or negative force on the development of Third World nations. You may also conclude that globalization has both some positive and some negative effects. Whichever perspective you take, be sure to defend your answer using examples and arguments from the viewpoints.

Chapter 3

1. Howard W. French states that, despite setbacks, there are reasons to be optimistic about the spread of democracy in Africa's developing nations. Ike Oguine, on the other hand, maintains that there are obstacles to democracy's growth in Africa. What issues do both authors see as problematic in Africa's developing countries? Based on these authors' arguments, do you think democracy is working in Africa? Why or why not?

2. William Ratliff maintains that the stability of governments in Latin America has kept true democracy from blossoming in the region. Omar G. Encarnación states that the stability is a sign that democracy is persisting in Latin America. Whose argument do you find more convincing? Explain why.

3. Anwar Ibrahim and Hilton L. Root refer to the Asian economic crisis of the late 1990s as a significant factor in the spreading or halting of democracy in that part of the developing world. How does each author use the crisis to further his argument? Do some research on the crisis and decide how you think its aftermath is affecting democracy in Asia.

Chapter 4

1. Comparing the arguments of Andrew Natsios and Larry Diamond and that of Neil A. Englehart, do you think the Millennium Challenge Account is a good way for America to distribute aid to the Third World? What are the strengths and weaknesses of their arguments? If you believe that the MCA is not a fitting means of distributing aid, what method of aid distribution would you advocate?

2. Considering the articles by Paula J. Dobriansky and John S. Sorenson, do you think it is America's responsibility to export democracy to Third World nations? Why or why not? How can developing countries benefit from democracy and the rule of law? How can the United States benefit from Third World democracy? Be sure to cite examples from the articles when answering these questions.

3. How much of the U.S. budget do you think should be spent on aiding the Third World? Taking into account the various recipient organizations (such as the Global Fund for AIDS) and goals (such as poverty elimination), how should that money be spent? By preferring some organizations and goals over others, do you think observers would criticize you for missed opportunities? How would you respond to them?

Organizations to Contact

Association of Third World Studies (ATWS)
Department of History
  Mississippi State University
  Mississippi State, MS 39762
(662) 325-7078
Web site: http://itc.gsw.edu/atws

ATWS is the largest professional organization of its kind in the world. With a global membership and chapters in South Asia and Africa, members include academics, practitioners in the area of Third World development, employees of government agencies, and diplomats. The association holds international conferences and publishes the *Journal of Third World Studies, ATWS Conference Proceedings, ATWS Newsletter,* and the *ATWS Area Interest List.*

Association for Women in Development (AWID)
215 Spadina Ave., Suite 150
  Toronto, Ontario M5T 2C7
  Canada
(416) 594-3773 • fax: (416) 594-0330
e-mail: awid@awid.org
Web site: www.awid.org

AWID is an international membership organization committed to gender equality and a just and sustainable development process. AWID facilitates a three-way exchange among scholars, practitioners, and policy makers in order to develop effective and transformative approaches for improving the lives of women and girls worldwide. AWID publishes *AWIDNews,* a quarterly newsletter that keeps members in touch with changes at AWID and in the global women's movement. It includes reports on recent events, thought pieces on critical issues, upcoming events, and advocacy updates.

Cooperative for Assistance and Relief Everywhere (CARE)
151 Ellis St. NE, Atlanta, GA 30303-2439
(800) 521-2273
e-mail: info@care.org
Web site: www.care.org

CARE is one of the world's largest international relief and development organizations. It works to provide basic education for children, economic and social empowerment for women, a stable supply of food and clean water, basic health care, universal immunization of children, and access to family planning services. CARE publishes an annual report and special reports on topics such as Afghanistan, AIDS, and India.

International Monetary Fund (IMF)
700 Nineteenth St. NW
   Washington, DC 20431
(202) 623-7300 • fax: (202) 623-6278
e-mail: publicaffairs@imf.org
Web site: www.imf.org

IMF's purpose is to promote international economic cooperation, to help keep a balance of trade among nations so that all benefit from the expansion of trade, and to lend its member nations money when necessary. It acts as a depository of information and statistical data regarding the economic affairs of its members. The fund publishes pamphlets, brochures, fact sheets, the semimonthly *IMF Survey*, and an annual report.

Millennium Challenge Corporation (MCC)
875 Fifteenth St. NW
   Washington, DC 20005
(202) 521-3600
e-mail: web@mcc.gov
Web site: www.mca.gov

Formed during the administration of George W. Bush in 2004, MCC proposed a new mechanism for delivering aid to developing nations who demonstrated a commitment to good governance by adhering to the rule of law, investing in the citizenry, and encouraging economic freedom. This aid disbursement account would provide U.S. aid in addition to other government channels that already provide relief monies. The organization's Web site lists eligible recipient nations as well as fact sheets and testimonies concerning MCC's mission.

North American Congress on Latin America (NACLA)

38 Greene St., 4th Fl.

New York, NY 10013

(646) 613-1440 • fax: (646) 613-1443

e-mail: nacweb@nacla.org

Web site: www.nacla.org

NACLA is an independent, nonprofit organization that provides policy makers, analysts, academics, organizers, journalists, and religious and community groups with information on major trends in Latin America and its relations with the United States. The core of NACLA's work is its bimonthly magazine *NACLA Report on the Americas*, the most widely read English language publication on Latin America.

North-South Institute (NSI)

55 Murray St., Suite 200

Ottawa, Ontario K1N 5M3
Canada

(613) 241-3535 • fax: (613) 241-7435

e-mail: nsi@nsi-ins.ca

Web site: www.nsi-ins.ca

NSI is the only independent, nongovernmental research institute in Canada focused on international development. The institute's research supports global efforts to strengthen international development cooperation, improve governance in developing countries, enhance gender and social responsibility in globalizing markets, and prevent ethnic and other conflicts. Its publications include books such as *Human Security, Sustainable and Equitable Development: Foundations for Canada's International Policy*, briefing papers, special reports, and speeches.

Organisation for Economic Co-operation and Development (OECD)2001 L St. NW, Suite 650

Washington, DC 20036-4922
(202) 785-6323
e-mail: washington.contact@oecd.org
Web site: www.oecd.org

OECD is a collective of thirty industrialized nations who discuss internal trade policies and assist nonmember, developing nations in boosting economic growth. OECD publishes more than two hundred books, journals, and information databases each year. Select titles include *Fostering Development in a Global Economy, Managing Aid,* and *Environmental Fiscal Reform for Poverty Reduction.* Many documents can be downloaded from its Web site.

Population Council

1 Dag Hammarskjold Plaza, 9th Fl.
New York, NY 10017-2220
(212) 339-0500 • fax: (212) 755-6052
e-mail: pubinfo@popcouncil.org
Web site: www.popcouncil.org

The Population Council is an international nonprofit institution that conducts research on medicine, social science, and public health. Focusing on developing countries, the Population Council works to improve family planning and reproductive health services and to study the causes and consequences of population growth. The Population Council publishes the *Policy Research Division (PRD) Working Papers* and the periodicals *Population and Development Review* and *Studies in Family Planning.*

United Nations Development Programme (UNDP)

1 United Nations Plaza
New York, NY 10017
(212) 906-5317
Web site: www.undp.org

The United Nations was established in 1945 to, among other things, help nations cooperate in solving international economic, social, cultural and humanitarian problems. The

UNDP engages in global advocacy and analysis to generate knowledge about—and develop policies to—aid developing nations. UNDP's primary areas of interest are democratic governance, poverty reduction, environmental protection, sustainable energy, gender issues, HIV/AIDS, information and communication technology, and crisis prevention and recovery. Numerous reports and facts sheets on these topics are available on the UNDP Web site.

U.S. Agency for International Development (USAID)
Ronald Reagan Bldg.
  Washington, DC 20523-1000
(202) 712-4810 • fax: (202) 216-3524
email: pinquiries@usaid.gov
Web site: www.usaid.gov

USAID is the U.S. government agency that implements America's foreign economic and humanitarian assistance programs and provides assistance to countries recovering from disaster, trying to escape poverty, and engaging in democratic reforms. USAID is an independent federal government agency that receives overall foreign policy guidance from the U.S. secretary of state. The public may look up and order USAID documents, reports, and publications by using the agency's online database of one hundred thousand USAID technical and program documents.

The World Bank
1818 H St. NW
  Washington, DC 20433
(202) 477-1000
Web site: www.worldbank.org

The World Bank is the world's largest source of development assistance, providing more than $17 billion in loans to its client countries in 2001. The bank publishes many books and reports on the economies of the developing world, including *World Development Report, Reducing Poverty on a Global Scale,* and *Globalization, Growth, and Poverty.*

Bibliography of Books

Haleh Afshar, ed. *Women and Politics in the Third World*. London: Routledge, 1996.

Surjit Bhalla *Imagine There Is No Country: Poverty, Inequality, and Growth in the Era of Globalization*. Washington, DC: Institute for International Economics, 2002.

David Bigman, ed. *Globalization and the Developing Countries: Emerging Strategies for Rural Development and Poverty Alleviation*. New York: CABI, 2002.

Judith C. Blackwell, Murray E.G. Smith, and John S. Sorenson *Culture of Prejudice: Arguments in Critical Social Science*. Orchard Park, NY: Broadview, 2003.

Lael Brainard et al. *The Other War: Global Poverty and the Millennium Challenge Account*. Washington, DC: Brookings Institution Press, 2003.

Peter Calvert and Susan Calvert *Politics and Society in the Third World*. New York: Longman, 2001.

Roderic Ai Camp *Democracy in Latin America: Patterns and Cycles*. Wilmington, DE: Scholarly Resources, 1996.

Noam Chomsky *Turning the Tide: U.S. Intervention in Central America and the Struggle for Peace*. Montreal: Black Rose, 1986.

Rekha Datta and Judith Kornberg, eds.   *Women in Developing Countries: Assessing Strategies for Empowerment.* Boulder, CO: Lynne Rienner, 2002.

Larry Diamond and Marc F. Plattner, eds.   *Democracy in East Asia.* Baltimore: Johns Hopkins University Press, 1998.

David Dollar and Lant Pritchett   *Assessing Aid: What Works, What Doesn't, and Why.* New York: Oxford University Press, 1998.

William Easterly   *The Elusive Quest for Growth: Economists' Adventures and Misadventures in the Tropics.* Cambridge, MA: MIT Press, 2001.

Susan George   *The Debt Boomerang: How Third World Debt Harms Us All.* Boulder, CO: Westview, 1992.

Anthony Giddens   *Runaway World: How Globalization Is Reshaping Our Lives.* London: Routledge, 2003.

Howard Handelman   *The Challenge of Third World Development.* Upper Saddle River, NJ: Prentice-Hall, 2005.

Jeff Haynes, ed.   *Towards Sustainable Democracy in the Third World.* New York: Palgrave, 2001.

John Isbister   *Promises Not Kept: The Betrayal of Social Change in the Third World.* Bloomfield, CT: Kumarian, 2001.

Carol Lancaster — *Transforming Foreign Aid: United States Assistance in the 21st Century.* Washington, DC: Institute for International Economics, 2000.

Jerry Mander and Edward Goldsmith, eds. — *The Case Against the Global Economy.* San Francisco: Sierra Club, 1996.

Michael Mason — *Development and Disorder: A History of the Third World Since 1945.* Hanover, NH: University Press of New England, 1997.

Martin Mowforth and Ian Munt — *Tourism and Sustainability: Development and New Tourism in the Third World.* London: Routledge, 2002.

John Mukum Mbaku and Julius Omozuanvbo Ihonvbere — *The Transition to Democratic Government in Africa: The Continuing Struggle.* Westport, CT: Praeger, 2003.

Daniel Osabu-Kle — *Compatible Cultural Democracy: The Key to African Development.* Toronto: Broadview, 2000.

Marina Ottaway — *Democracy Challenged: The Rise of Semi-authoritarianism.* Washington, DC: Carnegie Endowment for International Peace, 2002.

Robert Pinkney — *Democracy in the Third World.* Boulder, CO: Lynne Rienner, 2003.

Robert Pinkney — *The Frontiers of Democracy: Challenges in the West, the East and the Third World.* Aldershot, Hampshire, UK: Ashgate, 2005.

Jeffrey D. Sachs   *The End of Poverty: Economic Possibilities for Our Time.* New York: Penguin, 2005.

Mitchell A. Seligson and John T. Passe-Smith, eds.   *Development and Underdevelopment: The Political Economy of Global Inequality.* Boulder, CO: Lynne Rienner, 1998.

Amartya Sen   *Development as Freedom.* New York: Anchor Books, 2000.

James Raymond Vreeland   *The IMF and Economic Development.* New York: Cambridge University Press, 2003.

Marilyn Waring   *If Women Counted: Worth and Value in the Global Economy.* San Francisco: Harper and Row, 1988.

Joseph N. Weatherby et al.   *The Other World: Issues and Politics of the Developing World.* New York: Longman, 2002.

Ernest J. Wilson III   *The Information Revolution and Developing Countries.* Cambridge, MA: MIT Press, 2004.

Paul A. Wilson, Josh Ruxin, and Agnes Binagwaho   *Combating AIDS in the Developing World.* London: Earthscan, 2005.

World Bank   *Globalization, Growth, and Poverty: Building an Inclusive World Economy.* New York: Oxford University Press, 2002.

Index